THROUGH THE SHADOW

MW01287315

DERMATOMYOSITIS AND MY WALK WITH GOD

Dear Mary,

Thank you for purchasing this. I pray this helps in your own experiences and walk with God!

David R. Coleman, MPAS, PA-C

RWB Publishing, Cheyenne, WY, USA

Books may be purchased at Amazon.com

RWB Publishing
Cheyenne, WY, USA

Book Layout © 2016 BookDesignTemplates.com

Through the Valley of the Shadow: Dermatomyositis and My Walk with God/
David R. Coleman, MPAS, PA-C. -- 1st ed.
ISBN 978-1-7356017-2-4
Library of Congress Control Number: 2021924412

Dedication

It is with all sincerity that I dedicate this book to my loving wife, Karen. When two young individuals get married, they rarely understand the responsibility portion of the wedding vows they cheerfully recite at the ceremony. To "love, honor, and cherish in sickness and in health…"

When my illness came and left me bed-bound and hospitalized, my wife rose to the occasion and began working through the difficulties that presented. She found ways for me to eat when I couldn't chew solid food and swallow it safely. She helped me move from bed to chair and from wheelchair to toilet without complaint or discussion. In spite of her own bad back, she lifted me from one place to another at risk of additional pain to herself! And she did it without question! She drove long distances to spend time with me when I was in the hospital and the nursing home.

Whatever need arose, Karen worked tirelessly to ensure needs were met and life continued for me and our family! She could have easily said, "Sorry, but this is too much for me." But she didn't. Neither of us knew what condition I would be in at the end of all this, but she stayed anyway! She showed her unending love for me by honoring the vows we exchanged in our youth! I would not have survived without her by my side!

Forward

In the Spring of 2015, I experienced a sudden, debilitating illness that left me unable to care for myself. The warning signs were very subtle and only became evident a few weeks before the full effects of the disease appeared. Within 1-2 weeks of the onset of my symptoms, I was unable to get around without assistance and I was no longer able to perform my job; patient care in urology.

I am well versed in medicine and have been healthy my entire life. The symptoms I experienced, and the speed with which they ravaged my body, was something I had never seen before. Even my colleagues were amazed at the pace of my decline! This was not due to an injury or ingestion of some odd food or chemical. Nor was this the result of a bacterial or viral infection. This was the result of an autoimmune condition. My body decided to eat itself, and my muscles were on the menu!

I needed to stop my body from continuing down this fatal course! I needed to become well again so I could continue to work and pay my bills. I needed to find a way to give my friends and family (and myself) hope that I would eventually make it through this overwhelming life challenge! I needed answers I could trust!

This book describes the challenges I faced and the spiritual (and physical) journey I experienced along the way. Though I had been a Christian all my life, I never really understood the complex questions, such as "Why do bad things happen to good people?" "Where is God during difficult times?" "Why doesn't He get us out of tough situations quickly?" "Why doesn't everyone get healed?"

Through my illness and my reading of the Bible, God showed me several "epiphanies" which answered those questions for me, and more! I can now apply my Christianity to my daily living easier than before. I do not have issues with those "challenging questions" as I once did. The experience of dying helped me to understand better the purpose of living!

I tried to describe the events in this book exactly how they happened. Sometimes I did not have access to writing utensils (or the ability to use such tools), so I had to rely on my own recollection or the recollection of others. Many (though not all) of the names in this book are fictional to provide a bit of anonymity for those involved. I know who they are and, believe me when I say, I am profoundly grateful to those who came to my rescue when I or my family needed support. I am also thankful for those healthcare employees in the clinics, hospital, and nursing home who went above and beyond to improve my health and get me back on my feet. Every one of them told me they were just doing their job. But they did it in a manner that always made me feel special! From the bottom of my heart, I say; "Thank you!"

I hope this book helps you to see God's hand in your life like He showed me in my life. I hope it helps you to grow in your faith and knowledge of God and the wonderful part He has for you to play in His divine plan. I hope this story helps bring you peace during your trials and tribulations. Thank you for taking the time to read this book.

CONTENTS

CHAPTER ONE

The Tables are Turned

Dawg! I never expected to need so much physical help in my life, especially as a healthcare provider. As a physician assistant in Urology, I was always the one on the giving end--treating patients, consoling those in need, and trying to make their time in the hospital as pleasant as possible.

Yet here I was, April 20, 2015, being admitted to the hospital because I was having difficulty swallowing and walking. Four weeks earlier I had taken a flight to Austin, Texas to give a lecture at a Urologic conference. I used public transportation while I was there and walked often. The only issues I had were the tissues around my eyes were a bit puffy, and I had difficulty reaching far around my back.

After I returned home, I began to have problems walking. I first noticed it while at my local supermarket. I was waddling like a drunk trying not to look drunk. My upper body was leaning back, and my steps were deliberate, wide, and slow. My legs would swing out a bit before planting in front of me to complete my stride. I stared at myself, wondering what inspired such a change in my walking style. I tried to walk "normal" but normal suddenly felt very abnormal to me. I couldn't get my body to coordinate my steps like it used to.

Then, in fairly rapid succession, other problems began to occur. The next night, while emptying one of our cats' litter boxes, I found I couldn't carry the bag of cat litter (28 lbs.) and walk to the trash can easily. Instead, I had to put my wife's cane under the litter bag and take only short, waddling steps. I also began to have limited range of motion in my shoulders. My right arm could barely raise up high enough for my hand to touch the top of my head. My left arm, though better, was only mildly better.

In the clinic (two weeks before my admission), I noticed other weird behaviors. I recall taking an exceptionally wide berth as I walked around an exam table and wondering, "Why did I do that?" I showed my gait to one of my urologist co-workers, and he said, "Yeah. I think you have something wrong." I called my family practice doctor and got in that very Friday for an evaluation. That same week, while waiting for his appointment, I began to have swallowing difficulties. Things would get easily past my tongue but would stop short of my esophagus. It would require additional swallowing efforts to get it down further. A mild annoyance initially, but it got more bothersome later.

Friday, I went in to see Dr. Mark Condor. He had been my family physician for several years and was well acquainted with my general health. He was smiling and shaking my hand when I started off, "Doc, I'm in trouble." "What do you mean?" he said, giving me a brief once-over look and not seeing anything out of place. "I mean I'm in big trouble!" I went on to explain my issues, and the more I spoke, the more serious his face became. After a thorough exam, he said, "Well, there are a number of muscular wasting diseases that can be caused by your medication or can come up out of the blue. We'll need to order some lab tests to get a better idea of what is going on specifically with you."

The next day, I went to the lab to have my blood drawn. This was the first day I found myself in need of a cane to get around. It was very foreign to me. Though I had been diagnosed with diabetes, high blood pressure, and high cholesterol several years earlier, I only had to take oral medication for my illnesses and never had to undergo surgery or anything else that would interrupt my ability to work or play any way I desired.

Now I was showing my shortcomings to the world. I was less than 100%. I was impaired and everyone could see it. I had suddenly become "handicapped," and I had no idea why. There was nothing I could point at to launch an attack against. I mean, I wasn't in an automobile accident from which I would have to spend time in healing. And this wasn't the result of a football injury or other sports debacle. This was happening to my body while I was in it, without any outside influences I could identify. And I had no idea how long this was going to last.

The following day my results came back. Most lab tests were within normal limits. One result, however, came back very abnormal. My Creatine Kinase (CK), a sign of muscle wasting, should have been between 30-174. It was 20,000! Several days later, it rose to 23,000! I immediately went online to find out more about it. One site mentioned a risk of renal failure with high CK levels. I looked at my Creatinine level (a marker of renal function). It was low, at 0.3. To help maintain my currently good kidney function levels, I increased my water intake over the weekend.

Monday, April 13th, I only worked half a day. Karen, my wonderful wife for over 30 years, drove me to work that morning and waited for me to end my day (since my work site that day was one hour from our home). I used a cane to walk into work but left it at my desk when walking into the exam rooms and when around patients.

Walking was getting harder to do. I contacted my home office and told them I would have to cancel any further clinics until my health issues improved.

The next day I was introduced to my Rheumatologist, Dr. George Washington (no relation to the first U.S. President, I was told). A thin, older gentleman, Dr. Washington had been practicing medicine for over three decades. Not too many things surprised him. He reviewed my lab results and gave me a complete physical exam. Noticing the dark rash over my knuckles, he said, "Yep. This appears to be Dermatomyositis. It's an autoimmune disease that attacks the proximal muscles-- your chest, back, abdominal, shoulder, and thigh muscles. They'll all begin to waste away. The good news is that with the proper medication, you can usually get back 50-100% of your prior function over time." Seeing the less-than-enthusiastic look on his face, I queried, "How much time?" "Oh, maybe in three to twelve months."

"I'm going to start you on prednisone and methotrexate. But you must understand something about this disease. This disease is like a runaway freight train, the medicines are the brakes, and we expect them to begin working right away. But you still have a lot of momentum going forward. We have to wait for that to stop before we begin to see signs the medications are doing their job. You will get worse before you get better."

"Worse before you get better?" I had to chew on that one for a while. How much worse could this get? I mean, I was already having trouble walking and I needed a cane everywhere I went. Because of the swallowing issues, I had to puree my food before eating it, and I could no longer sleep flat on the bed. My back had to be elevated to allow me comfort without choking on my own saliva. I was also having constipation issues and noticed my heart rate was elevated with the least amount of activity.

Karen set up a large wedge cushion on the living room couch and made a nice bed for me there. That elevated my head adequately for sleep. Another large wedge cushion helped elevate my legs as well (I was beginning to have swelling in my feet by the end of each day). Because I couldn't get around easily without assistance, she placed a large glass container next to my bed and I had a urinal within arm's reach. When I needed to urinate, I would do it discretely into the urinal while under a cover, and then empty the urinal into the glass container and replace the glass lid. Karen would then empty the glass container the next morning.

This system worked great (I initially thought). I could urinate as often as I wished, and I didn't have to disturb anyone during the night. But being alone in the living room allowed me the chance to think about my situation. Though we were creatively addressing my daily issues, this was not how I was expecting to live at this stage of my life. I expected to be physically well, able to lift whatever I cared to lift, and walk wherever I pleased. Yet here I was in bed, using a urinal because I was unable to safely get in and out of bed without assistance. And just last month, I was normal.

CHAPTER TWO

God in All of This

Another aspect I had to consider was my spirituality. As a Christian, I was taught that God is in control. So what was happening to me now? Was this some attack of the devil, as some would claim things like this to be? Was this a righteous punishment for a misdeed or disobedient act? Well, I always believed the Bible to be the inspired Word of God, and with a sudden amount of uninterrupted time on my hands, I decided it would be the best place to go to start finding my answers.

When looking up some of the qualities of God, I stumbled on Isaiah 46:9-10 where it speaks of God's knowledge, "Remember the former things long past, for I am God, and there is no one like Me, declaring the end from the beginning, and from ancient times things which have not been done, saying, "My purpose will be established, and I will accomplish all My good pleasure."" Jeremiah 1:5 states, "Before I formed you in the womb I knew you. And before you were born, I consecrated you..."

The Bible also describes His power and sovereignty in Psalm 103:19, "The Lord has established His throne in the heavens, and His sovereignty rules overall," and in Colossians 1:16, "For by Him all things were created, both in the heavens and on earth, visible and invisible, whether thrones or dominions or rulers or authorities – all things have been created through Him and for Him."

I found another interesting verse in Deuteronomy. When speaking about identifying a real prophet from a false one, the Bible says, "When a prophet speaks in the name of the Lord, if the thing does not come about or come true, that is the thing which the Lord has not spoken..." (Deut. 18:22). That means that all things that have happened have been allowed or approved by God. As I mentioned before, His purpose will be established.

So, if God knows "the end from the beginning," and He knew what was going to happen to me, then He knew about my Dermatomyositis early on. If so (I began to think), I wonder how early God knew about this happening to me? Well, the answer was, of course, from ancient times. Then my first big epiphany occurred to me--this illness was a surprise, but only to me! This was only a surprise to me! Though this was nowhere on my radar, God was aware of it from long ago. And if that was so, then it meant this illness was His "Plan A" for my life all along (my second epiphany)! My "Plan A," staying healthy and active and doing what I pleased, was nowhere in His plans for me this year. Making me immobile and dependent is where He wanted me to be.

This was particularly challenging for an independent guy like me to accept. I mean, I always thought I knew what was best for me and my life. And being dependent on others for basic things just didn't fit into my plans anywhere. Now, I could have acted like a petulant child acts when they don't get their way. I could have thrown a tantrum and argued with God. But I felt that would get me about as far as a spoiled brat gets with responsible parents. I needed to understand more about God and my relationship with Him to better get through all that was changing around me.

As I read further in the Bible, I came across Moses trying to get out of leading the Israelites out of Egypt. He tells God that he has a stuttering problem (as if God didn't already know). God's reply is found in Exodus 4:11, "The Lord said to him, "Who has made man's mouth? Or who makes him mute or deaf, or seeing or blind? Is it not I, the Lord?"" And in John 9:1-3, the Bible speaks about a blind man's healing. "As He passed by, He saw a man blind from birth. And His disciples asked Him, saying, "Rabbi, who sinned, this man or his parents, that he would be born blind?" Jesus answered, "It was neither that this man sinned, nor his parents, but it was so that the works of God might be displayed in him.""

I slowly began to realize that this isn't a matter of "good versus evil" as watching two opposing forces on a battlefield. God is in control of all things! Lamentations 3:37-38 states, "Who is there who speaks and it comes to pass, unless the Lord has commanded it? Is it not from the mouth of the Most High that both good and ill go forth?" As described in Colossians 1:16, "…all things have been created through Him and for Him." God controls all sides, all players. Nothing is done without His approval or allowance. Nothing (epiphany #3)!

The thing that often warps our minds is, God grants us all free will, yet He knows the choices we will make in our future (already made in His knowledge) and the thoughts and desires that brought us to those choices. And all our choices (past, present, and future) are incorporated into His plans! He doesn't "guess" how things are going to happen. Everything in our future has already happened in His past. He knows the future because it's past tense for Him.

"Well," you might say, "if everything that has happened in the past has been within God's plans, why have there been bad things in the past?" I believe that is the difference between God's plans and God's will. In my youth, I was taught John 3:16, "For God so loved the world, that He gave His only begotten Son. That whosoever believeth on Him should not perish but have everlasting life." This verse explains Biblically how someone can be saved from sin and spiritual death. This is an excellent example of God's plan. But it's the very next verse that sheds light on God's will. "For God sent not His Son into the world to condemn the world, but that the world through Him might be saved." (John 3:17)

God's will is that the entire world would be saved from sin and death, and everyone would voluntarily follow Him. But He gave us free will and many have chosen to turn away from God and do whatever they desire. In doing so, they have brought about bad choices and undesirable results. Because God knows all the choices we will make freely in our lives, that has been incorporated into His plans. And His plans will be accomplished!

This revelation was very comforting to me. In knowing that God controls everything, I only need to seek God whenever any challenges come my way (epiphany #4). I needn't worry about another individual or entity "messing up" God's plans. I know that whatever is happening to me is allowed by God for my instruction, training, discipline, correction, or all of the above. I just have to keep my focus on Him!

Karen later reminded me about Psalm 23. Verse 2 states, "He makes me lie down in green pastures, He leads me beside quiet waters." "I wonder if this isn't one of the ways He brings you to the green pastures and still waters," she said. "It's like He says, "Here are the green pastures" and "Here are the still waters." And like the numbskulls that we are, we usually respond with, "Thank you, Lord, for that nice bit of information. I, however, am going over here, where my life/work/friends are and I'm going to get a few things done." Then God hits us with something like Dermatomyositis and says, "You don't understand. I'm making you lie down in this green pasture. Trust Me. There will be nothing more pressing in your life right now than getting close to Me and finding rest."

That seemed to be how it went for me. I mean, without the muscles to move my body around, I could do no work. With the swallowing and constipation issues, I had to focus on simple things just to get through each day. No longer did I think about all of the lofty thoughts every other adult ponders through their day. I was now focused on such matters as "Do I have equipment easily available to me in order to urinate without assistance?" And I thought, "God, surely You don't want me hobbling around like an invalid, do You? I mean, I don't get it." I was basically saying that since this physical change was not part of my "Plan A," I'm sure it couldn't remotely be part of His "Plan A" either.

Then I read in 2 Corinthians 12 where Paul, the Apostle, was fighting with a "thorn in the flesh." In verses 8-9, he describes imploring the Lord three times that it might leave him. "And He said to me, 'My grace is sufficient for you, for power is perfected in weakness.'"

So, knowing that God is always in control, and that His plans always come to fruition, it was easy to say this was indeed His "Plan A" for my life. My job was to get on board...or not. "Or not" seemed like a very foolish move to make. I mean, we're talking about God Almighty. The Creator of the heavens and the earth. The One who knows the end from the beginning. As my muscles were rapidly deteriorating, I was becoming more frail with each passing day.

Because so many different things were happening to me physically, and since I knew God controlled all things, someone asked me months later if I was ever "mad" at God? Throughout my entire ordeal, being mad at God never crossed my mind. I think the main reason we get mad at God is that He didn't use our "Plan A" as His "Plan A." We wanted to remain completely healthy or we wanted our family member to live longer. We were OK with God having total sovereignty, so long as He followed our plans.

Romans 9:20-21 describes our relationship with God as clay with the potter. So to be mad at God would be like clay getting mad at the potter because the potter wanted a plate instead of the ornate figurine the clay itself desired to be. Clay doesn't have a right to get mad at the potter, and neither should we presume to have a right to get mad at God.

Another verse came to mind, Hebrews 9:27, "...It is appointed for men to die once and after this comes judgement,..." Knowing I had nothing to do with the planning of that upcoming appointment, once it happened, my next waking moment would be standing before the judgement seat of God Almighty as He pondered over the final destination of my eternal soul. Now, suppose that time came while I was still mad at God? I would be risking my eternal salvation on a temporary physical disagreement with God. And not accepting His "Plan A" willingly, also seemed like the epitome of foolishness.

Romans 8:28 says, "And we know that God causes all things to work together for good to those who love God, to those who are called according to His purpose." Though I've quoted this verse for years, it recently occurred to me that no one quotes this in times of prosperity. You quote this in times of trials and tribulations because it's during those times we want to be reminded of God's uplifting promises. No matter how terrible things look at present, God will make it "work together for good" for His followers. No such promise exists for those who fight God every step of the way.

So knowing this was God's "Plan A" for my life coming to fruition in the "here and now," I resigned to accept it and work with God anyway He saw fit. I felt comfortable in the palm of His hand and under His total control. I prayed that He would grant me the strength to get through each day and the ability to give Him glory regardless of what issues came my way. It was important for me to maintain my focus, since after being on immuno-suppressive medication for about a week, my little "freight train" was nowhere near the end of its momentum-driven journey. I had lost fifty pounds of muscle mass in three weeks' time. My health continued to decline.

CHAPTER THREE

First Hospital Stay

I realized I was getting worse. Since first meeting Dr. Washington about two weeks earlier, my swallowing was unimproved, my standing ability was very weak, and I was getting more constipated with each passing day. As a runner has a slow heart rate to show how healthy his body is, my heart rate continued to climb anytime I had to apply the least amount of exertion, suggesting just how fragile the state of my health was. We decided the time had come to take me to the emergency room.

Though April 20th was a Monday, and it was about 10 a.m. when I arrived, the ER was almost empty of any other patients, so I was immediately shown to a room and promptly evaluated. Dr. Jackson reviewed my recent labs and my medical history. "Your CK levels are really high," he said, trying to calmly put things in perspective. "We usually get concerned when they get above 10,000." "Yeah. That happened about 10,000 points ago," I countered.

Later, after having consulted with my Rheumatologist, Dr. Jackson informed me they were going to check me over for cancer while I was admitted, since there was a small known association of Dermatomyositis and cancer. So, away I went for an MRI of my brain, CT scans of my chest, abdomen, and pelvis, and more lab tests. A swallow study was also performed to see just how problematic my abilities had become.

Having spent most of my adult career in medicine, the hospital setting was extremely comfortable to me. I've never been seriously sick before, so being on the receiving end of all the scanners and other machines took some getting used to. I understood the need to check for associated diseases, so I wasn't too nervous about discussing cancer right off the bat. Karen focused on me and tried to make sure I was comfortable. My adult sons, Brian, and Nathan, were in unfamiliar territory, so they appeared to just be processing their surroundings and the fact that I was the patient and not the provider.

The nice thing about my condition was I didn't have any pain issues to speak of. My problem was in the rapid muscle wasting throughout my body. Because my muscles had deteriorated, they were unable to move my bones. So standing became more challenging each day. My heart muscle also suffered from wasting, so my pulse rate elevated to compensate.

My diaphragm took a hit as well, so I felt mildly short of breath over time. I also found that I could no longer cough. It seemed like such an easy task before my illness. Now, the best I could hope for was to clear my throat ("with enthusiasm," I often explained). And my gastrointestinal (GI) tract began to slow down a bit, causing me to have swallowing and constipation problems.

Someone asked me months later if I ever thought about crying out to God because of so much going on with my health? In all honesty, I felt less desire to "cry out to God" and more a desire to understand what He was taking me through. To that end, talking to God in prayer was definitely in order. I prayed and read my Bible much more earnestly during my illness. But I always felt God was with me through this, so I didn't need to "cry out" to Him as if He were beyond my sensory range.

I just had to remember that God is in absolute control, and He promises to "cause all things to work together for our good..." (Rom. 8:28). My job was to let God know I had total trust in Him and was willing to go through whatever He required, so long as He went with me.

Too often, we focus only on the physical things around us and lose sight of our spiritual support. As Psalm 23 states, "Yea, though I walk through the valley of the shadow of death, I will fear no evil: for Thou art with me... (vs. 4)." "For Thou art with me!" That phrase really spoke to me. I didn't have to worry about anything happening to me because God was with me! He was the creator of "the valley" and everything in it. He knew the path I was about to take. I really didn't feel anxious or afraid. And I never needed to "cry out" to Him because He was already there.

I've heard others say, "God, if You heal me from this disease or take this trial from me then I'll follow You." But I believe God wants us to follow Him first, regardless of the trial we're facing. He doesn't want us to barter with Him, placing our selfish desires over His plans. He wants us willing to do what He asks. "To obey is better than sacrifice ..." (Isa. 15:22).

One of my favorite stories in the Bible is of David and his battle with Goliath (1 Sam. 17). It's not just the story of a young man winning over a much larger foe, it's a story about understanding proper perspective. The Philistine army was on one mountain and the Israelite army was on another mountain with a valley between them. Goliath, an exceptionally tall and strong monster of a man, stepped into the valley and challenged Israel to a duel. If whoever they sent out beat Goliath in a one-on-one fight to the death, then the Philistines would become servants of Israel. But, if Goliath beat Israel's warrior, then Israel would become slaves to the Philistines. This challenge gave the advantage to Goliath, as there was no one in the Israelite army of comparable size, and Goliath would most assuredly win against any single challenger.

Well, no one in the Israelite army responded. You see, the trained warriors in the Israelite army were staring at Goliath and hiding in their tents in fear. They saw Goliath's massive frame, strong muscles, and heavy armor, and could not find a weak spot anywhere on him. They examined themselves and found they were lacking the strength to compete against such a beast. So they did not challenge him.

King Saul also looked at Goliath's physique and knew he had no one in his army to compare to Goliath. So he hid in his tent as well. He was so desperate over the whole situation, he let the young, inexperienced David challenge Goliath, since he was the only one willing.

When Goliath saw David come out to meet him for the challenge, he saw a young man with no visible warrior attributes anywhere! He knew he could take David and crush him with little or no effort.

What did they all have in common? They only saw the physical aspects of their situation. David was the only one to see the spiritual side. He wasn't weighing his own strength and training against his adversary. He didn't really care about Goliath's armor or fighting experience. David knew that God was by his side and would take care of Goliath!

Was David just "hoping" for a good outcome? No, this was a young boy who had no doubt. When you are heading to your death, you usually walk very slowly in hope that an alternative might arise before your time comes. David was so excited to see God take care of Goliath, he ran out to meet him (vs. 48)! And David made sure to let Goliath know that he was facing God Almighty that day, and not just a young untrained shepherd boy.

And what is it we fear when we "cry out to God?" Is it dying? Illness? Pain? Deformity? Remember, God is in control of all things! And all physical things are temporary. Picture yourself in a room with an angry, violent man who has a gun pointed at you and his rage is extreme. Who has control over whether you live or die? You? Obviously not. You have no weapon, and he has the gun pointed at you ready to fire. Does he have control? No. He, like everything else everywhere, answers to God! He may be mad as a wet hen, but unless God wants to use him to bring you into eternity, nothing he does is going to end your life. Nothing! It's entirely up to God.

Now, instead of an angry man with a gun, suppose cancer is the angry adversary who stands before you? Again, who has control over whether you live or die and when? Is it the cancer? No. Because even cancer has to bend to the will of God. It doesn't have to have a brain in order for God to control it. He told the Red Sea to part, and it did (Exodus 14:21). Jesus told the water to hold Him up, and it did (Matthew 14:25). He also told the wind and the waves to be calm, and they did (Mark 4:39). Cancer may eventually be the manner in which God has you leave the earth and enter into His presence, but that decision is up to Him, not the cancer! And remember, "…It is appointed for men to die once and after this comes judgement,…" (Hebrews 9:27). "AND AFTER THIS…!" The end of your time on earth has no relation to the end of your existence! God has eternity planned for you and me! Our time on earth is brief in comparison.

That's what I mean by keeping a spiritual perspective on things. God may take you through trials, tribulations, and things you might find unpleasant but know that He watches over His children and causes all things to eventually work out for their good.

CHAPTER FOUR

My Next Challenge

After my tests were completed, a room was prepared for me on the fourth floor. An IV was also started and high-dose steroids were initiated to help with my immuno-suppression. I was still getting around with a cane, and they would periodically walk me around the ward for exercise.

In spite of my best attempts, I was still quite constipated and unable to have a bowel movement. My anus was sore from trying, and I mentioned my plight to Mary, my nurse. I was thinking she might recommend an enema or stronger oral medication to address the situation. "Well, let's just lay you down on the bed and disimpact you right now," she calmly stated. This really didn't sound appealing to me, but I knew I was running out of options and was feeling quite uncomfortable from it. "OK," I said.

She promptly laid down some chux on the bed, had me lay on my left side, slid my pants down to my thighs, and said, "This might feel a bit uncomfortable." Boy, was that ever an understatement! She pushed her gloved finger through my already sore anus and dug around my rectum for impacted stool. After bringing out what she could, she then reinserted her finger and dug around for more. I now had a new "10" level for that 1-10 pain scale everyone talks about. My colon then began to move enthusiastically, and stool migrated quickly from the right side of my abdomen over to the left side and then down to her awaiting finger. And each finger reinsertion brought on my anal pain all over again.

The whole ordeal only took one or two minutes, but it felt like I had tumbled down a very steep hill, always striking it only on my anus! My body was spent, and my anus was beyond sore. I laid on my left side and just groaned weakly. "I think we're done," Mary cheerfully said. "How are you doing?" "Just tell me you got some stool out of there," I groaned. "Oh yeah. I got out quite a bit," she replied. "Do you want me to leave you in this position for a while, or get you moved onto your back?" "This position is good for now," I said, not sure if I had any energy left to support a move. She then placed a pad soaked in witch hazel on my anus, covered me over and left the room.

I don't think I've ever felt that tired and abused before in my life. "Rode hard and put up wet" was the term that came to mind. If someone had come into the room right then and killed me, I couldn't have felt worse. I just laid there in silence and tried to regain whatever strength I could.

I probably should have felt embarrassed over the whole ordeal, but I truly felt too numb and fatigued to care. We adjust our modesty barometer according to the level of seriousness of our condition. If it's a small bone break or a minor rash, our modesty remains intact. If our major systems begin to fail, we're more open to such indiscretions, if they will solve our current problems. And when you find yourself unable to have a bowel movement, it doesn't take long before you're willing to do about anything to get relief.

I eventually felt better and was able to enjoy my family's company when they checked in on me. My doctor had me on an IV and most of my medications changed over to IV since my swallowing was becoming more difficult. Soup went down easiest for me, but anything firmer needed to be pureed. Because of the high-dose steroids, my blood sugars went all over the place. Instead of remaining under 140, they would range anywhere from 120 to 380, even if I ate the same things. Because of this, I began insulin injections multiple times each day. I also had to have finger-stick blood sugar checks before every meal and at bedtime. That, coupled with lab testing most mornings, made me feel like a pin cushion in no time flat. My fingers, arms, and abdomen quickly came to detest the daily ritual.

The next morning, before it was even light outside, a technician came into my room and woke me up. "Hi. My name is Lori and I just need to get a little blood from you." "OK," I said, adjusting my eyes to the light. Lori, like most phlebotomists, was a study in efficiency. She placed her little hand cart down near her and put a small tourniquet around my upper arm. She looked briefly over a few areas and promptly found a vein that pleased her. "Little pinch," she said as she pushed the needle past my skin. In no time at all, she had several vials of blood collected. She removed the needle, placed a gauze over the needle site, dressed it, and said goodbye, outing the room light on her way out the door. Everything happened so quickly, I could have almost slept through the entire visit.

About a half hour or so later, the ward began to come to life. Soon a technician came in to check my blood sugar and my vitals (blood pressure, pulse, respirations). Then, around 7 a.m. the night nurse and the day nurse would make their rounds to introduce the incoming staff. I got a few minutes alone after that to get ready for breakfast. Usually, the day nurse would get there right before breakfast to give me my insulin injection and any oral medications due at that time. If all went according to plan, my breakfast would come around this time, when no other visitors were expected.

Being able to eat in peace and watch the news became a cherished respite from other normal ward activities. I also felt better eating alone, since my swallowing issues forced me to concentrate more. Due to my diminished reach, I needed the staff to set up my tray with everything in easy reach. I also needed to be in a chair as opposed to my bed when eating. This allowed me to feed myself by placing my arms on the arm rests and bending my elbows until my hands gained easy access to my mouth. Without my elbows starting out on high arm rests, I wouldn't have the strength to lift my arms high enough to touch my face. If everything was set up just so, it provided me a feeling of accomplishment to feed myself without spilling anything. It also gave me a small sense of independence as well.

Sometime in the morning, either before, during, or after breakfast, the doctors would come by and talk about my current symptoms and their plans for my immediate future. I would see the hospitalist who was standing in for my family practice doctor and my rheumatologist, any specialists consulted to my care which became numerous as time went on, and then the specialty technicians would also visit throughout the day. For me, it felt a bit like being in my own "Christmas Carol" with one ghost following shortly behind the other.

CHAPTER FIVE

Ambulatory Support

During my initial stay in the hospital, I was still getting around with just a cane, but that changed to a walker fairly early. While walking down the hallway with Joan, my physical therapy technician, I found that I could no longer push down on a cane and get adequate "push back." Because my muscles continued to break down, I no longer had the strength to push the cane into the ground for support. I remember her propping me up against a wall, making sure my knees were locked and I was in a comfortable standing position, and going to get a nearby walker to use. I found I didn't have the strength to push fully against the walker either, but I did have enough strength to remain upright with it. I would glide it across the ground and then lightly hold it with my fingers as my legs walked into it. As long as I kept my head up and looking forward, everything went well. It balanced me better than just using the cane alone.

I got to experience a second disimpaction several nights later when my bowels failed to empty as planned. I had been sitting on a toilet for a while without success. By the way, I was now considered a fall risk, so anytime I was out of the bed or wheelchair, I had to have an attendant with me at all times. That meant no more using the restroom by myself. When I mentioned to Rhonda, my RN attendant, that I was having trouble, she asked if I needed another disimpaction. I said "I think so. Should I get back on the bed?" "No," she said. "Just lean over your walker and we'll do it right here." With that brief direction, she slipped on a glove, bent me over the walker, and proceeded to dig stool out of me like looking for expected change from a vending machine.

All I thought about was trying to stay on my already wobbly legs without falling down. After she was satisfied she got out what she could, she sat me back down on the toilet to rest a bit. She stepped out of the bathroom to give me a bit of privacy. I remember whimpering quietly to myself and praying, "Lord, out of all the things that have happened to me so far, if You could just keep my bowels going well, I'd really appreciate it."

A third disimpaction occurred two days later, though I was placed in bed on my side for that one. It wasn't as rough as my first or second ones were, but I was glad when it was over. I think the disimpactions were the most challenging activities I had to endure during my stay in the hospital.

The foods that I ate were primarily soft foods. I did well with things that were mushy, such as apple sauce, mashed potatoes, soup, and yogurt. Things that were harder and required chewing were more likely to get stuck in the back of my throat. Even scrambled eggs became more difficult for me, especially if they were dry, because the flakes would get away from me and lodge just past my tongue. I began taking my eggs over-easy and in a bowl. It allowed me better control when feeding myself. When taking pills, I found it best to take them with yogurt. I could mix them into the yogurt, and they would swallow just fine. Trying to swallow pills by themselves was just unbearable. Anything that got stuck in the back of my throat forced me to continue with swallowing attempts until the item moved on.

Without chest muscles, I found I had lost the ability to

cough. This was worrisome for me because I couldn't rush myself when trying to clear my throat, for fear it might go down my windpipe and really cause me problems. One morning, after I had received breakfast, Gina, the nurse of the day, came in to see how I was doing. I told her things were well and I was looking forward to the day. She said she would leave me to my breakfast and walked out of the room. Not 10 seconds later, I took a bite of toast and turned my head when I heard something out in the hallway. Well, the bite of toast lodged just above my windpipe and didn't allow me to breathe. Without the ability to cough, I was having an extremely tough time trying to move the piece of toast aside. I quickly rang my call bell and continued to try and clear my throat. After a quick look, I realized no suction was set up in my room, either. I was finally able to clear my throat after 40 seconds of continued trying. Gina came back about a minute later.

I explained what happened and that I would like to have a chaperone present for all of my future meals. I also wanted suction set up in my room. Gina agreed and changes occurred immediately. They also scheduled me for a swallow reevaluation.

It was interesting to see what activities I could no longer do from day to day. Where early on I could walk easily around the room, later I began to rely on the walker more and more for stability. My arm strength and reach also diminished almost daily. I had to be mindful about the types of food I ate, so as not to risk choking on something hard to swallow or to increase my risk of constipation again.

I remember telling one of my nurses, "When someone asks you what's normal for you, you immediately have an idea in your head. That's not the way with me. Every day

I have a decrease or loss in mobility or activity. My "normal" changes daily." When someone would ask me if I could do a particular task, I found myself thinking, "Well, I could do it yesterday. But today, I'm not so sure." So every time I performed a task, I would either smile thinking, "Hey, I can still do it," or I would frown thinking, "Well, there's another task I'm no longer able to do or at least do easily."

I could no longer predict what my physical body was capable of doing. Simple tasks, hard tasks. They all needed to be attempted before I could be confident in my physical skills. My mental skills were, however, untouched by my condition. I knew and understood everything I knew before. Since I was the one in the family who managed the bills and other routine paperwork, I started compiling things together and making notes so that Karen would be able to take things over if I became unable to address these items. It's funny what you think about when your health deteriorates. Not appreciating just how far my health would diminish, I thought about what would be needed to keep the bills being paid and everything in its place.

For Karen, doing the bills did not come easily, so me sending her home with tasks related to keeping track of, or even taking care of, the bills was very unpleasant. She was also the leader of our church's Women's' Ministries and carried a load of responsibilities for that position. She drove from home every day to visit me and take care of me. She never liked driving long distances and my hospital was almost an hour away by freeway. This just added to her overall stress, but she was by my side every moment she could be.

CHAPTER SIX

Rehab

After the first week in the hospital, I remember waking up on a Saturday and feeling a bit stronger in my legs. I told my hospitalist that I might have come to the point where my "locomotive has stopped moving and started to reverse." It was a mildly perceptible change, but a change, nonetheless. Though still getting multiple medications and injections for immuno-suppression and my other conditions, they transferred me to the rehab ward on the fifth floor to focus primarily on getting me ready to eventually go home.

Rehab was really fun. On the main floors, the focus was medicine. So most of the activity was happening in my IV and through my oral and injectable medications. Yes, the nurses took care of my daily needs, but they didn't mind leaving me alone for extended periods of time when I had no special requests. Rehab was planned activities two or three times a day. They had a board set up on the wall and each night they would write the schedule for the next day on it. Usually it would consist of one hour of physical therapy, one hour of occupational therapy, and one hour of speech/swallow therapy. Throughout the week, they also threw in a shower and general physical testing.

Though I had been in medicine for many years, I was never in a specialty where I had to interact with rehab, so all of this was unfamiliar to me. How it was explained to me was that physical therapy (PT) works on getting you moving on your own, and occupational therapy (OT) works on your ability to do things once you're where you want to be. In other words, PT works your lower extremities and walking issues, and OT works your upper extremities and hand/eye coordination issues. Being now fifty-five pounds lighter than when I was admitted, everything needed work since I had lost significant muscle mass.

My first full day on the rehab floor proved to be quite busy. Joan, from PT arrived at 9 a.m. just as scheduled. She promptly began to evaluate my leg strength and mobility to see what we might be able to do. Then she got me out of bed and walked me down the hallway with my walker. She took me to the main PT room, commonly referred to as "the gym." It had long, padded, tables set to chair height that allowed one to sit on them and even lay on them while having your muscles worked. Pulley systems were also around to increase your shoulder range of motion--ROM--and strength. They had stairs there and even a car replica to practice getting in and out of vehicles. Coupled with recumbent bicycle machines and other "tools of the trade," this was one state of the art facility.

Farther down the hall was a kitchen with an island to allow you to work on placing and removing things from shelves, and on getting around routine kitchen obstacles. I was also shown a bathroom that had been modified to allow training to get in and out of bathtubs and to use bathroom helps. It was also set up for wheelchair access. I was quite impressed! You really never think about what you need to perform a task until you can no longer do it "the normal way." After running me through a routine of exercises and walking around the place, she delivered me back to my room just in time for my OT session.

Jennifer, my OT tech, was a very pleasant 30-

something-year-old. She examined my current upper body strength and ROM before taking me over to the gym for light exercises. I still couldn't easily get my hands to reach my face, so we did more ROM activities. After the gym, she brought me into the training bathroom and we went over tooth brushing and face washing, not so much how to do them, but how to perform these tasks with limited strength and range of shoulder motion. I quickly learned that simple tasks were simple no longer. I had to use a long handle with a sponge at the end when I wanted to wash areas like my back and shoulders, places my hands alone could no longer reach. I could brush my own teeth, but only in my wheelchair where my arms could remain upright by using the arm rests.

Following right after my visit with OT, Sidney and Gail came by from Speech/Swallow therapy to evaluate me and work on therapy regimens for me. They brought along snack items similar to what they used during my swallow study. They wanted to formally go through the foods to better assess my current swallowing ability. Sidney said Gail was "learning the ropes" of Speech Therapy and was here to help. Being a medical provider myself, I told her I understood the need to train someone, and I was fine with having her there.

They began by giving me soft food items, such as apple sauce and peanut butter, to see if I had any difficulty with them. They proved to be easy to swallow, as expected. Then they graduated to flakey items, like crackers and chips. These were more difficult for me to manage and required several swallowing attempts before they moved down my esophagus. When the sample pills came out, they performed no better. The capsule shape took multiple tries to resolve. The other pills did OK, but still did not go down easily.

Following the swallowing trial, they then hooked me up to a muscular stimulator--or TENS unit--and began to stimulate my neck muscles. It delivered timed shocks to the pads stuck on my neck. This helped strengthen the muscles that remained in my neck. I was told this might improve my swallow ability quicker. It felt like leaning your neck against an electric grip tester at an old carnival, though lighter in intensity. It did gradually make my neck feel better. Swallowing, however, didn't change much during this time.

Sidney then showed me exercises to improve swallowing. "First," she said, "try pushing your tongue onto the roof of your mouth while you swallow. That may help." I tried it and I think it did help a bit. Then she placed a rolled-up ace bandage under my chin and had me squeeze it against my neck for a count of ten. We did that exercise several times. Then she had me stick out my tongue when swallowing. After seeing myself in the mirror doing these things, I started to crack up. "It's the weirdest thing," I informed her, "to voluntarily learn an involuntary action." "I mean, nobody thinks about swallowing. They just do it! To have to tell your body how to swallow is just a hard concept to wrap my head around." We all laughed.

They planned to be there around the start of lunchtime, and lunch came right as expected. All of my lunches consisted of soft foods, such as soup, mac and cheese, mashed potatoes, and jello. It was also diabetic-friendly, so very low on sugar. The ladies watched me start eating and left when they were satisfied I was doing OK swallowing everything. Since my swallowing had improved from early in my stay, I was OK with eating by myself now. As long as I was given sufficient time to swallow my meal without rushing, I usually did fine. Forty minutes was what I hoped for as a minimum. If I had to eat faster than that, I felt nervous getting things down efficiently.

One morning, my PT time was scheduled with "Music Therapy." This consisted of a technician skilled in guitar, harpsicord, and other solo instruments playing songs around a bunch of us patients. We would move a given extremity in a directed fashion in order to build muscle strength. Stuart was his name, and he sang songs I was familiar with, songs of the 70s and 80s, James Taylor, Simon and Garfunkel, John Denver, and the like. Whatever sounded right for a campfire setting worked for PT. Being musical myself, I felt obliged to sing along in harmony with Stuart. I really had fun doing the exercises and singing along. When the hour was over, it was time for lunch, and we were taken back to our rooms. I found out quickly that, after singing, my vocal cords had a tough time allowing food to go down like it should. I had fatigued them too much. After that, I made sure never to sing around a planned mealtime.

CHAPTER SEVEN

Free Time

After the planned activities and scheduled mealtimes, they would usually leave us patients alone to do whatever we desired. Karen would usually try to stop by each day and catch me up on the happenings outside the hospital. She had taken on the monumental task of collecting the bills, keeping the house and property clean and orderly, keeping up with a little collectables booth we had in our hometown, and meeting all of her personal obligations as well.

While together, we'd go over each other's day and what mail she brought. Though my day was fairly routine, hers would consist of getting calls from her sisters back east, meeting with the women of our church for bible study and going around the city in her daily tasks and informed me about who she met along the way. It was nice to hear normal things each time she came: Who she had seen and what they said, what my cats had done to her (and the house) the night before. Just regular things helped remind me that I had a normal life waiting for me "out there." That helped inspire me to keep up with my exercises and get better soon.

My brother John, who's retired and living in the Denver area, also came by to visit. We don't usually talk much, but that's because we both have busy family lives and our paths rarely cross. But once we meet, we talk like we'd recently been together. Anyway, I caught him up on my condition and how my healing was coming along. He (as well as most of those who met me) had never seen anything like this. I was using a walker, was quite a bit thinner and weaker than he was used to seeing and needed support to aid me with my daily activities. But I helped him understand my spirits were high and I was in otherwise good condition. It was good to reconnect with him, and he made it a point to come by whenever he had the chance. Since I was an hour south of Cheyenne, that also made it less of a trip for him to come see me.

When I was alone and my visitors were away (or had yet to arrive), I would type a bit on Facebook and keep my friends aware of what was going on in my life. Since many of my friends were PAs like me, I wanted them to understand my rare disease and what it can do to a body. Most of my high school friends still live in California, so I also wanted them to know about my current adventures. Facebook was a great forum for getting the word out easily.

The response back was overwhelming. Many wrote to express their concerns and support. Some informed me they would pray for me at their locations. Others told me they were gaining spiritual strength reading my posts. I myself felt I was beginning to understand God and my walk with Him better through dealing with this disease.

Knowing God was in control of all things kept my focus on God throughout this time. Though my body was wasting away, and I was relying on others more than I ever had before, He let me know He held me in the palm of His hand and would help me grow spiritually during this time. Truthfully, this ordeal was working out for my good, and I could see it happening daily. Most of us, if we had something bad happen to us and knew who caused it, would be angry at the source of our calamity. But when it's God and we understand He's doing this for our spiritual benefit, we come out of our ordeal praising God and feeling blessed for the challenge. I was in the worst physical shape that I had ever been in my life, yet I was gaining spiritual strength daily!

And I understood that God gave me strength through multiple ways. The more I read the Bible, the more He began to show me how He interacted with Israel and His desires for His people. He also gave me strength through my Christian (and, oddly enough, my non-Christian) friends. They would either give me words of encouragement or tell me what God was doing to them and for them through my Facebook postings. By them describing strength they acquired from my posts, it gave me renewed strength as well.

A few days after my visit with John, my brother Tony showed up for a visit. Now this was totally unexpected. Tony lives along the Pacific coast of Washington State, so he rarely ventures out to my neck of the woods. Seeing him walk into my wardroom was quite a surprise. John came along and we had a good time getting together and talking about things. I didn't realize it then, but John had called him and told him if he wanted to see me alive, he should fly out soon and visit. I laughed about it later, because at that time, I felt I was still looking well overall.

I eventually began to improve in mobility ever so slightly. I remember telling Dr. Washington that "I think the train has finally come to a stop." I still had difficulty ambulating without a walker (and sometimes even with one), but I was beginning to swallow better. He decided that if I continued to improve over the next few days, he would send me home.

They tried different ways to improve my physical and occupational therapy. Denise, from PT, came by and, with an assistant, would get me sitting up on the side of my bed. They then brought over a rolling lift and would have me place my feet on the platform. My arms would then grab a hand bar in front, and together we would hoist me up until I was in a standing position. Then I would lock my knees and they would put the seat down behind me. Once on the seat, the unit could be moved to another part of the room easily. And as long as someone watched my head position, I was able to travel this way without a problem.

Denise would often have me go from a sitting to standing position in the unit and hold it as long as I could before sitting again. They would assist me with a gait belt to get from one position to another. Even so, this slowly began to rebuild my leg muscles.

My brother-in-law Harvey, who lives in Michigan, heard what was going on in my life. He was retired and fairly well off. He had time to go places and the resources to take him anywhere he desired. He called and told me, "Dave, if you want, just say the word and I'll have a jet come pick you up and take you to the MAYO clinic." "Harvey," I said, "I'm at a state-of-the-art facility right here and they're taking very good care of me. Plus that, I work for this organization. It would look weird if I chose to leave here for a hospital out of state."

CHAPTER EIGHT

The Calm Before the Storm

As promised, I was able to leave the hospital on May 6th, 2015. Per routine hospital protocol, I was taken to my car by wheelchair. I was thankful for that since I still had difficulty walking with a walker. They stopped the wheelchair close to the passenger door, so I was able to stand and get into the car with minimal effort. I thanked the staff for helping me during my time in-house. Then we headed home.

It was nice finally getting away from the hospital environment. The drive home felt almost new to me, though I had taken that road every working day over the last 3 years. It was late afternoon, but still light out. The grass seemed greener, the air fresher, and I was happy putting the hospital in my rear-view mirror. Upon arrival home, Peter, one of my dear friends, came to help me get out of the car and into the house. A fairly simple task since I had some mild strength left.

Karen had cleaned up the living room and my cushions were placed so I could sleep on the couch easily. We also had a small recliner couch I had bought a while back at the local thrift store placed in the dining room in case I wanted to relax there. Several antique hotel desk bells were placed throughout the first floor to be ready in case I needed help.

She made a small work area for me in the dining room on the first floor. I had a small adjustable bedside stand with my computer on it, and nearby was a pedal and hand crank machine, in case I wanted to exercise my extremities. A pulley system was fixed to the wall so I could extend my arms out as wide as possible and work on my shoulder range of motion.

She had made our home as comfortable and wheelchair accessible as possible. I could get anywhere on the first floor in my wheelchair. I only needed my walker when I was going to the bathroom. It was a basic walker without any frills, but it worked for my needs. Suzanne and Kim, two dear friends, came by later and surprised us with a rolling walker with a cushioned seat and storage area. It was fantastic! I could get through narrow areas too small for my wheelchair without much problem.

The first evening back at home, I decided to try and sleep on the recliner set up for me in the dining room. A bell was placed near the seat in case I needed anything during the night. Karen tucked me in as one would a child. Then she kissed me goodnight and went to her room.

It was somewhere around 1:30 a.m. when I began to get uncomfortable with the thrift store recliner. I sat up and considered my options. I figured the best course of action was for me to wheelchair over to the living room and crash on the couch for the rest of the night. Though my wheelchair wasn't far from me, the cushions I normally had on it were in separate areas of the dining room. The seat cushion was a few steps to my left. The back cushion was on the dining room table ahead of me. A neck pillow I wanted to use once I got on the couch, was on a buffet table about seven or eight steps ahead of me. No big deal, I thought to myself. I'll just use the furniture for support, and I'll be done in a jiffy.

I went for the seat cushion and had no trouble

retrieving it and getting it on the wheelchair. Then I got the back cushion in place without much additional effort. The neck pillow was my last task but when I got to it, I realized I was beginning to lose strength. My head leaned forward as I used the dining room table for support. I could feel myself quickly losing the ability to stand. Then, without warning, I went down. I wasn't able to guide my descent or prepare myself for the fall, I just fell.

The weird thing was the fall didn't hurt at all. And somehow, the neck pillow wound up under my head and I hit the floor on my right side in an almost fetal position. Not a bone was broken, and I was feeling comfortable on the floor. This was good, because I had no ability to move my extremities or change my position in the least. But being on my right side faced me to the living room and the rest of the house. I knew I was going to need Karen's help to get off of the floor. I figured it might take a while to get her attention, so I started calling her name. But one of the muscles affected by my condition was my vocal cords. I couldn't yell. I could barely get above a whisper. But I kept calling out her name, nonetheless.

It wasn't five minutes later that I heard her come out of her room. "Well," she exclaimed, surprised at my predicament. "What happened to you?" I explained my situation to her and told her I was comfortable, no need to call an ambulance. We thought about things for a minute and decided to leave me on the floor. She set pillows around me, got my water glass and urinal within easy reach, and left a desk bell near me. We figured if we waited until the morning, we could call someone over to help get me back in the wheelchair.

That worked for about three hours, and then I began to get uncomfortable. I called her back and said we needed to try getting me back into the wheelchair. This was not going to be easy, what with her bad back and my inability to provide any reasonable assistance. Then I got an idea. If she altered between lifting my bottom and then my head, she could use pillows to slowly get me high enough to get me into a chair. Karen agreed.

She started by lifting me by the waist belt. This got my butt off the ground high enough for me to slide a large pillow under me. Then she would add a pillow to my head, and we would get another pillow under my butt after another quick waist belt lift. Eventually, I was high enough to slide a small foot stool under me. Then she got a taller stool under me and eventually I was high enough to make it back into my wheelchair. The entire process took about an hour and a half, but it safely got me off the ground and didn't put too much strain on Karen or her back. From that point on, I decided not to get up out of anything without someone else present.

I usually kept a gait belt on me to help when transferring me around. Once I had my arms around Karen's neck, she would grab me by the gait belt and stand me up. I could then lock my knees and would have minor risk of falling. I would then shuffle over to the wheelchair and she would help me to sit down. As long as I held her around her neck or grabbed her forearms, we did well standing me up. Without good neck muscles, sometimes--actually most times--my head would fall forward on the lift and I would bury it into her shoulder. Then we would straighten my glasses after I made it to the wheelchair.

It started being easy to assist me into a standing position. But within a day or two, it became more of her doing the lifting and me supporting the effort less and less. Sometimes it took two or three "hikes" to get me up high enough to lock my knees. This was especially true getting me off of the toilet. Toilets, in general, are much lower to the ground than the average chair. That low center of gravity, coupled with having to pull my pants up before I could sit back down, made the toilet a challenging lift.

As you can already tell, Karen was a trooper throughout my ordeal. When standing at the aisle exchanging vows, we often say such things as "for better or worse, for richer or poorer, in sickness and in health" without fully thinking about what those words might entail. After all, we're both usually healthy and strong and exhibiting no obvious signs of weakness.

But when something serious comes our way, that's when our vows are truly challenged. I suddenly found myself without the ability to support myself in the least. Karen looked after all of my daily needs without even a brief hesitation! She took over tasks I no longer could address and was still able to maintain all of her own personal obligations. She honored her vows in spades!

CHAPTER NINE

Uncle Charlie

Amidst the challenges of losing many of my routine abilities, I got a call from my Uncle Charlie. Uncle Charlie had been a Christian for years. He had been a devoted Bible-believing, "always in church" kind-of guy. But several years ago, he got caught up in a "name it and claim it" type of church in his local community. He was even involved in their healing ministry on Tuesdays. This is where they would receive sick and infirmed individuals and pray over them for healing. If healings didn't occur, they would often say that the individual "just didn't have enough faith."

This is an area where he and I disagree regarding what the Bible says. In regard to faith, Ephesians 2:8-9 says, "By grace you have been saved through faith, and that not of yourselves, it is the gift of God, not as a result of works, so that no one may boast." In other words, God gives us faith to be saved, so that no one can say "I'm just more faithful than you, brother." God said faith is not from a result of one's works, so one can brag about it.

I told Uncle Charlie that I felt he was putting himself in an unbelievably bad position. "What do you mean," he asked? "Well, the problem I have with you "name it and claim it" folks, is that one day you're going to tell someone they "just don't have enough faith" for whatever it is they desire, and they're going to believe you. They're going to say, 'Wow. That's all the faith I can give, and it's obviously not enough for God.' Then they are going to turn their back on God, and you will have just contributed to the loss of a soul!" "At that point, the Bible says, 'it would be better for you to have a millstone hung around your neck and be cast into the sea.'" (Luke 17:2).

I continued, "The physical is temporary. The spiritual is eternal. Jesus didn't come to heal the sick. Matthew 1:21 says he came to 'save His people from their sins." Uncle Charlie felt that physical healing was just as important as spiritual salvation. He thought that Satan was the one who made people sick and that he operated against God's will. I quoted Exodus when God told Moses, "Who makes him mute or deaf, or seeing or blind? Is it not I, the Lord?" (Ex.4:11).

He felt that was a misquote and that God really didn't make anyone ill. "Look," I explained, "if you keep your eyes focused on the physical, you'll find you're looking in the wrong place. You need to focus on the spiritual. Let me give you an example: Owning a mansion is one way of showing success in the world's eyes," I began. "And whenever you see mansions in commercials or on one of those reality shows, they're usually surrounded by well-manicured lawns and have expensive sports cars or limos in the driveway. Now, granted, anyone of them could hold Bible studies in the facilities, but that's not what's usually shown. More commonly, the folks there are shown holding parties and engaged in some self-gratifying activities." "So what?" he chided.

"Well, where, IN REAL LIFE, do you see Christians AND non-Christians focusing on God, praying to God, examining their own mortality, and otherwise thinking about their relationship with God? That is usually at hospital and nursing home bedsides, next to cemetery plots, at accident sites, and such. Those activities we think of as "bad," God uses to refocus our attention on Him and our relationship with Him." I went on, "You can see God describe this kind of activity all through the book of Judges in the Bible. God entered into an agreement with the Israelites and shortly after, they began following other gods. He then sent in their enemies to punish them and then they would cry out to God. He would then hear their cries and bring them out of bondage. Then they would have peace until they disobeyed God again."

Uncle Charlie again would not agree that God could allow illness to remain. He felt that physical healing was of foremost importance to God. I realized I wasn't making much progress with him, so I finally said, "OK. You want to go there? Let's go there. Tell me something, when Jesus healed folks in the Bible, do you think He had enough faith to heal them?" "Yes," he said. "He did." "And when He healed them," I continued, "Do you think He healed them completely?" "Yes, of course," he quickly replied. "Great," I countered. "Let's call one of them up and see how they're doing. Oh, wait a minute… THEY'RE ALL DEAD!" I said emphatically!

"No matter what kind of physical healing happened to them, they all eventually died. That's because the Bible says, 'It is appointed unto man once to die, and after this the judgement.'" (Heb.9:27) "Consider that a promise from God, a promise with an appointment!" "Do you recall making that appointment," I continued? "No. God made the appointment. And when did He make it? Well, way back when time began. So He has first dibs on the date and time." "So when that time comes, trust me, your plans are going to be interrupted and His plans will come to fruition."

The only thing that matters in this life is our choice to

accept the free gift of salvation from Jesus Christ and to follow after God Almighty. Nothing else matters! Invent a cure for cancer? Nice, but not relevant when standing before the judgement seat of Christ. Discover a way to end world hunger? Great! It still has no bearing when standing in judgement. Biblically speaking, this will not be a matter of your good actions outweighing your bad ones. The Bible states "All have sinned and fallen short of the glory of God." (Rom. 3:23.) Our good actions "are as filthy rags." (Isa. 64:6.) Our salvation is not dependent on any good works we can do or our ability to be kind. Our salvation from sin only comes from Jesus Christ.

CHAPTER TEN

And So the Storm Begins

During the day, I worked hard to keep the bills straight and to fill out medical forms associated with my illness and time away from work. I also wanted to cut my monthly bills quickly, so that if I had to take a medical retirement, we could still keep up with expenses. So I began the process of refinancing the house.

The first call was simple. But after that, forms began coming in the mail requesting all kinds of personal information and document copies. That took a while to compile. Over the course of the next few months, we'd send completed forms back to them and then they would send over another group of forms to fill out, some identical to previous forms completed. As I got sicker, Karen was tasked with completing things and returning them. Financial forms and documents were not her forte, and it often frustrated her how they wanted to know every nuanced detail of our lives before they would approve the deal.

Being retired Air Force and now primarily confined to a wheelchair, I submitted paperwork to the VA in hopes of changing my status from "abled" to "disabled." This also required completing forms, though they were primarily on the internet. When I finally got to speak to a representative, they informed me that to be considered disabled from a VA standpoint, I had to have acquired my illness while in the military or during combat. Other than that, I was still 100% "abled." It seemed an odd statement since I needed people to help me do everything.

Harvey, my brother-in-law, was concerned about my well-being, so he and his wife Kora drove down from Michigan to see if they could help me out. Karen was happy having her sister and brother-in-law here for support. It did, however, add a mild bit of stress because Karen is a hostess and feels obliged to wait on house guests whenever they're here. That, coupled with my frequent needs, put a bit of strain on her.

Harvey is a go getter and once he got here, he immediately started looking at what he could do to make the place better for me. Our house wasn't handicapped accessible, so he considered options to improve my entrance into the house. The hardest part for me was from the front door to the car. There are two large concrete steps to navigate and with a wheelchair, it was easier to have two guys just pick me up (in the wheelchair) and carry me over to the car. But with just Karen and I, we'd have to call people over to get me in and out of the car.

Another problem that came up shortly after Harvey arrived was that my reliable SUV wouldn't start. This was very uncommon for my car and couldn't have come at a worse time. Harvey made this issue go away. He took the car to the dealership and had them work the whole thing over. Kora stayed with us and took us to my appointments in her van.

In spite of everyone's best help and support, I continued to worsen. My arm strength and range of motion declined. My leg strength weakened as well. I continued to puree all my foods, and any oral medication I took had to be placed in yogurt to get it down. My bowel movements were difficult to express without me manually assisting myself. And transitioning me from one seat to the next was done primarily without any help on my part.

I recall taking a casual assessment of my overall health and realizing my body was losing quite a bit of muscle and function. If things continued to deteriorate, I could easily die before my medication stopped my disease process. I mentioned this observation to Karen, but she didn't believe things were that far along. "You still have a lot of kick left in you before we remotely begin to think about such things," she replied. Since it was only a brief concern, I figured she was probably right.

On May 21st, Karen and I went to the outpatient physical therapy clinic and met Kathy for the first time. She got me onto a large flat table and tried to get me to move. Other than moving my hands and feet, nothing else budged. Then she hooked me up to a ceiling hoist that allowed my legs to walk underneath it. Once it got me up, and as long as someone kept my head upright, I was able to move my legs and propel me forward. Karen even took a short video of the event.

After that, I was sent to Dr. Matthews, the physical therapy doctor to get an outpatient evaluation. She looked me over a bit and then reviewed my records. "You look like crap," she casually said. "I think I need to get you back into the hospital." My original thought was, "No way! I'm not doing too bad right now." But the more I thought about it, the more I realized she was right. I was in bad shape. "I tell you what," she began. "Stay in your car. I'm going to call Dr. Washington and get his opinion of you before I make my decision."

So we went back to the car and stayed in the parking lot while she figured things out. It was about 10 minutes later when she called and said orders were waiting for me at the hospital. So we went directly to the hospital (same parking lot), and I started my second stay that evening.

CHAPTER ELEVEN

My Home Away from Home... Again

Once I got to the third floor and they found out I hadn't had a good bowel movement in several days, they promptly disimpacted me. I was beginning to think this was just the standard greeting for all patients upon admission, their way of saying, "Welcome to our facility," so to speak. It didn't hurt like my first disimpaction, but it was still rough work on an already beaten-up body.

Dr. Washington came by later and said he was going to start me on IgG. Immuno-globulin helps build your body back up. It's given to you through an IV, and since it has a large protein load, it's given to you over the course of 4 days. Because it costs about $25,000 a dose, they try to make sure you get every drop of the medication out of the bag before they discontinue it. The complete process takes about two and a half hours a dose to administer. I tolerated it very well.

I also stayed on high dose steroids and, because of my diabetes, had to begin insulin therapy. Also, because I was confined to bed and couldn't move much, they began to give me enoxaparin injections so to diminish my risk of forming clots in my legs. That coupled with morning lab tests and finger-stick blood glucose tests brought me back to "pin-cushion" mode.

The nurses and technical staff were all great helps for me. They were quick to address any needs I had; and in my condition, I had plenty. I couldn't reach my pillows, so

I always had to have someone adjust them for me before I tried to sleep. I knew how annoying this would be, so I tried to get one good adjustment before bedtime and left it like that until someone came in to do something else to me. They tried to change my position in bed every two hours. Being on my back was the most comfortable. But they also wanted me to spend time on my right side and then on my left side. Side positions were never greatly comfortable because I needed to have the head of my bed elevated to breathe better. On your side, this gave you the mild feeling of being a pretzel. But rules were rules, and the nurses did not want to break any rules.

Karen was beginning to have health issues due in part to all the different stressors placed upon her. In spite of that, she was good about coming to the hospital (an hour away from home) daily to visit me. She would catch me up with the happenings at home and she would be around when the doctors came by to speak with me. We didn't do anything special, but I enjoyed seeing her each day.

On the fourth day of my IgG treatment, she called to say she didn't feel well, so she wouldn't make it over that day. I'm not a very clingy person, but I really felt bothered that she couldn't come. She was providing me moral support and I had come to rely on it even more than I thought. Harvey came by instead and we had a chance to talk. He informed me that they decided to do a quick, but necessary, remodeling to the house to help get it ready for me when I returned. I knew there were things that needed attention; the garage roof had a hole in it, the basement needed some electrical work, the porch roof was also in disrepair, and the house was generally disheveled.

Being the hostess she is, I knew this would bother

Karen something fierce, having people going through our house changing things all around her. We also had several indoor cats that we wanted to make sure didn't get outside. But Harvey felt he knew what needed to be done, and he came well-funded for the task.

He saw that my yard had trees needing attention, and the side of my house was a small graveyard for old lawn mowers. So, while at a local hardware store, he met a group of Spanish landscapers and hired them right on the spot and had them drive over and start working on the side of my house and the back yard. I would have thought it would take several days of intense work to get my yard back in shape. But they brought their equipment with them and cleaned things up in 1 day. Amazing!

I also heard that my two sons and many of our church family came to help at the house. People brought pick-ups and trailers to move out the garage items and other stuff. Some cleaned rooms, some did construction, and others straightened things up. Harvey was most impressed with my sons and how diligent they worked. "Those boys became men in my eyes," he said with some reverence.

Later that day, Brian, my oldest son, his girlfriend Nam, and a church friend named Marshall, came by for a visit. It was nice to see them all. I mentioned to Brian what Harvey had said about him and he blushed a bit.

After Brian and Nam left, Marshall and I had time to talk. "You know, it takes a condition like this to see what kind of friends you have. I have people working on my house who hardly say much to me at church." "I know," he said. "You should see all the people who came out when they found out you needed help." "Marshall, I'm learning that God is in control of everything in my life, including this. If I just keep my focus on Him, he will show me why I'm going through this and what I need to do in all of this."

"I agree," he said. "Remember when I had my prostate cancer? Well, God brought my wife and I closer together and helped us see what really mattered in our lives." "And now, when I talk to someone going through a cancer scare, I can better relate to their issues and concerns, because I went through it, too."

"You know, when I do something for you, it's a linear thing. I do it for you and you receive it from me," I began. "But when God does something, it benefits all kinds of people. I mean, when I got this disease, it put me in a position to get closer to God and interact more with my wife. Because of that, this turned out to be a blessing for us. I also felt the need to write about it on Facebook. Next thing you know, I'm getting all kinds of comments about how my experience is blessing others in their trials. I was just amazed at how many people were affected by it."

The next day, I tried to have a bowel movement but was unsuccessful. The nurses promptly gave me another disimpaction that morning. Later that day, when I once again needed to go but couldn't, the nurse gave me an enema. When that didn't do the trick, they rolled me over and gave me a final disimpaction. Needless to say, I had my fill of disimpactions! So I started requesting bisacodyl tabs every morning to help keep me regular. Polyethylene glycol was also on stand-by in case I needed additional support. I was going to do everything in my power to avoid having any further disimpactions.

CHAPTER TWELVE

The "Interesting" Patient

With all of the immuno-suppressants I was taking, my CK levels began to drop. At the start of things, they were 23,000. In early May, they got down to 8,275. Now they were fluctuating between 2,490 and 2,851, with higher number being the most recent. Dr. Washington said I was the most severe case of Dermatomyositis he had ever seen. "You're a very interesting patient," I heard him say. He informed me that he would speak to a Dermatomyositis specialist he knows in Denver, to see if there was something else to do for me. I remember telling many of my patients in the past that "one thing you don't want to be is 'interesting' to the medical community." "That means they don't quite know what to do to you, but they'll 'try their best'."

Karen came by the next day and informed me of the happenings at home. "You'd think a bomb hit it," she fumed. "I mean, they tore apart our basement. OUR Basement! I wasn't having problems with our basement. Were you?" "Well..." I started but was quickly cut off. "And they ripped up the entire basement carpet and threw it out," she added. "It had been soaked many times in the past," I reminded her. "Oh, and they also found out one of our former cats were using an area behind the old octagonal couch as a poop center," she piped in. "There were several old mounds back there. I'm sure that's where that smell was coming from. Anyway, though it's in total disarray, the place smells much better now."

On May 27, 2015, Dr. Washington came to visit. After the usual chit-chat, he told me that he was going to start me on another IV medication tonight called Rituximab. It would be administered by two chemo nurses, and they would start with a low dose and ramp it up every half hour until I developed muscle pain. Then they would stop it. Of all the things I was going through and having to take, this seemed like just one more thing. No big deal. "Sure," I said. "Do you think it will help?" "Dr. Jones in Denver said it's a good drug and often can help turn things around."

Karen and I continued to catch up on the happenings at home. She was beginning to get frequent calls from the mortgage company, and they were sending more forms to complete. She was also getting stressed out with so many people moving around the entire house and taking things to different locations. It was also getting harder making sure the cats stayed inside. People were accidentally leaving the front door open and our cats were still small. Time spent in my wardroom became therapeutic for both of us. She would vent to me about things stressing her out, and I'd reassure her that God was in control and would take care of things for us. Then we'd breathe easier and just relax spending time together.

Late in the afternoon, Tami, and Mary, two chemo nurses came by and started bringing in the trays and machinery needed to start the Rituximab trial. They had me sign a treatment consent and then gave me a sheet of paper describing the medication in detail and all of the potential side effects (quite an extensive list, I might add). Karen asked if I wanted her to stay. "No," I said. "You go on home and connect with everybody over there. I'm in the capable hands of these two lovely nurses and this thing is supposed to take several hours to administer anyway." She agreed, gave me a kiss goodbye, and headed out the door.

I took a general look around while the nurses were getting ready. Everything seemed so surreal. A little over a month ago, I was working in the clinic without a care in the world. Now, I was in a hospital bed needing help to do just about everything. Since I had a moment, I got off a quick Facebook note describing my current situation and the med trial I was about to undertake. I think I ended the note with, "Well, here goes nothing."

CHAPTER THIRTEEN

My Early Demise

They attached a line into my present IV, and then described their procedure once again to me. "We're going to start with a very low dose. Every half hour, we'll increase the dose until we start getting muscle aches. Then we'll stop. This usually goes without a hitch and people tolerate it fairly well." "Great," I said. "We might as well get started. I'm not planning on doing anything else tonight."

With that said, they started the machine, and the medication began to flow. So far, so good. I really didn't feel any different than having regular IV fluid running. A half hour later, as promised, they asked how I was doing. "Fine." They took vital signs and increased the dose. Again, no changes in sensation or activity.

I believe it was shortly after the one-and-a-half-hour dose increase that things took a terrible turn. All of a sudden, my chest got really tight. It felt like I was being bear-hugged by a bear! Exhaling was OK, but it was very difficult to inhale. Then I remembered some of the side effects I read about. "I'm having a bad bronchospasm," I exclaimed! "I'm having a hard time breathing!" "I'm calling a code," yelled Mary. "I'll shut off the machine," said Tami. Someone got oxygen on me, but I wasn't feeling any better. "I need some EPI now," I barked! I thought if that doesn't help quickly, I'll soon go into respiratory arrest where my breathing stops, and then cardiac arrest where my heart stops beating.

It seemed odd that this morning I had a 30-year life

expectancy, and now I was staring at maybe a three-minute life expectancy! I took a few more breaths, but the Epinephrine didn't seem to help my breathing at all. That's when I realized, "Yep. I'm going to go into respiratory arrest and then cardiac arrest." It was like being strapped into the world's tallest roller coaster and coming to the end of the large incline before the first major drop. You know it's going to happen, and there's nothing you can do about it now. You just have to hold on tight and get ready for the ride.

The code team came into my room, pushing their equipment into every available space they could find. The leader, a critical care doctor, sat next to my bed and began talking to me. "David, I'm Dr. Thompson. How are you doing?" At this point, all I could get out was "bronchospasm" between my labored breaths.

He and his team worked around me trying to improve the situation. But I knew the statistics. In a first-rate facility like this, with an up-to-date code team at the ready, there was a 50% chance I would live through this code blue if I arrested. Outside the hospital, the percentage dropped to about 11%. And I knew a full arrest was exactly where I was headed!

But I wasn't really afraid at all. I looked at the team before me and thought they all looked like a bunch of bright bulbs. I'm sure they were going to do the best they could to keep me alive. But all they could do was their best. From them, there was no guarantees as to the outcome.

Instead, I felt an overwhelming peace from God, knowing He had total control over my life AND my death. In thinking that way, death wasn't really a big deal as much as it was a movement from one area into another. I wasn't thinking, "Oh my, I think I'm going to die tonight." Instead I was looking around thinking, "Oh, so this is how I go into eternity. How about that!"

Breathing was becoming more difficult. I remember praying, "Lord, if my dying helps someone come closer to You, I'm cool with that. And if living through this brings You glory and praise, I'm cool with that, too. Whatever You want of me, I'm ok with because I know You're in control over all of this." I remember Him saying to me, "Do you really believe that?" "Yes, I do," I answered. "Good," He said. "Then go take a nap." That's when my old military training kicked in, "Sir, yes, Sir!" I willingly replied.

I remember thinking that if I really struggled and fought it, I might get another one or two minutes of breathing, but I was very tired. So I picked a breath, I think it was the breath after I decided it, and I stopped breathing. I even said to myself, "OK. This is my last breath." Whatever was going to happen to me from this point on, was going to happen without any further input from me. Once I took that breath, I quit fighting.

Things slowed down at that point. I remember when it was time to take my next breath, it didn't come. If you've ever tried to hold your breath, that only lasts a short time, and then your body takes over and forces you to breathe. No such response from my body. It was like it was saying, "No. We're cool with this." Soon my head began to bob. I thought, "Well, I'm either going to wake up in a new location with a brand new, fully functional body, or I'm going to wake up back on earth and have to heal from all this. But I said, "whatever God wills," and I meant it. And with that thought in my head, I passed out.

It took about an hour for Karen to get home. It was evening time, so many of the church volunteers had already left for the day. Harvey and Kora began filling her in on what was going on throughout the house. The garage roof was being worked on. Several volunteer contractors were looking into what could be done to the porch to allow me better handicapped access without making my house look like a nursing home. The basement was in upheaval, but electrical work was being completed there. The cats had not gotten out of house. All were safe and accounted for. A call from the hospital came over her cell phone. "Hello, Karen, we need you to come back to the hospital right away." "OK," she said. "I'll be there as soon as I can."

The way the call was made worked out well. Since Karen had no clue as to why they wanted her back, she wasn't thinking about anything critical. She had an hour drive ahead of her, and had she been concerned about me, I think it would have made her driving extremely dangerous. But she last left me comfortable in my bed with two nurses at my side. At Kora's request she went with Karen and they headed directly back to the hospital.

On the way down, she got low on gas and had to stop in route. She had forgotten her credit card and had no cash on her. Kora had money, so she paid for the gas and the ladies resumed their trip. Karen later told me the first sign of something going wrong was when she got to the ER, the only door unlocked at that time. She was met by two chaplains. Instead of taking her to the third floor, where she thought I was, she was taken to ICU on the second floor.

At the nurses' desk, Amy, a nurse that had been working on me throughout my ordeal, filled her in on what happened. "After they called a code blue on him, he went into respiratory arrest. We worked on him for a while, and eventually got him on a ventilator on the third floor. While we were transferring him to the ICU, he went into cardiac arrest. We worked on him for over 20 minutes before we got him back. He's in the room behind you. We're just cleaning him up a bit." It was at this point that Karen passed out right in front of the nurses' desk.

Kora said she took a look in my room and saw a naked guy on the bed with tubes and wires going everywhere. I believe I wound up with two large-bore IVs in my arms, a central line in my neck, an interosseous line through my right tibia, and a foley catheter in place. I was also on a ventilator with an endotracheal tube down my throat. Oh, and I was still unconscious. They quickly called Harvey, and he came right over. It seemed bazaar how quickly I went from just "hanging out" in a wardroom to being a full code blue patient!

Later that evening, Karen took time to update our Facebook friends on what occurred. She wrote, "Hello, friends and family. It is 3 a.m. and I am here sitting with David Coleman in the Cardiac Intensive Care Unit (CICU). He suffered a cardiac arrest (code blue) at approximately 9 p.m. this evening and was given CPR for 25 minutes and paddle shock treatment to revive his heart. They are still trying to stabilize him as I write. We look to God as our refuge and strength and very present help in our time of need. His presence here tonight is very real and powerful, as mighty prayers have been lifted up all over the country for our Dave. They sustain us. They encourage us. They strengthen us and bring us peace. Thank you all for your continued prayers and support."

That note brought many responses throughout the US, from California to Maine. People sending kind words and expressing thoughts and prayers on our behalf.

Reading them later on, it was very humbling to see folks discussing personal changes in their faith through reading about our trials.

CHAPTER FOURTEEN

There and Back Again

When I awoke, I found myself with a tube in my mouth breathing for me and IV lines all around me. My very first thought was, "Dawg! No new body. Well, I guess I'm going to have to heal from this disease." But I quickly told God I was cool with whatever He decided, so I started getting it in my head that my focus now was on healing. This was going to be no easy task. I had no muscular structure to speak of and I couldn't even breathe for myself. Physically, my only benefit was that I had no real pain issues. I was, however, one weak waif of a guy.

Amy told me they were thinking about chilling my body down to preserve mental function, hypothermic therapy. But I woke up and started moving my finger like I wanted to write something on the bed. When they put their hand nearby, I started writing on their palm, "Cognition intact. Take pics." They thought that was funny, but I was thinking that when all was said and done, I wanted to see how bad I really got. Karen laughed about it later. "Yeah, I thought that after coming back from a code blue, your first words would be something romantic like, 'I love you, honey.' But no."

When I first started processing my situation, I felt the positive pressure breathing of the ventilator happening. It's a different kind breathing from normal "negative pressure" breathing and can be a bit unnerving early on. But I could see how God prepared me for this, because I was trained in positive pressure breathing while I was in the US Air Force.

In negative pressure breathing, it feels like we inhale and that expands our lungs, and we breathe. Actually, our chest muscles (and diaphragm) expand and create a negative pressure environment. Air then passively enters our lungs through our bronchi and that's how we breathe. Exhaling comes when the chest muscles and diaphragm relax, and air is expressed out. When parameters change, like in a fighter jet where 'G' forces are greater than our ability to overcome them easily, we'd never be able to guarantee each breath. So the pilot mask shoots air into our lungs, expanding our chest muscles and creating a positive pressure environment. We then exhale with force and prepare for the next breath. I received training in an altitude chamber once when I was thinking about getting an "incentive flight" in a fighter jet. Unfortunately, that opportunity never came for me, but the training finally paid off.

When the machine breathed for me, I understood right away what it was doing. So instead of trying to fight it, I just relaxed and began to synchronize my breathing with that of the ventilator. It worked great and was very easy to breathe with.

Since I was now alert, I wrote notes frequently in everyone's hands. If folks asked me yes or no questions, it was easier for me to respond. But if they needed me to be more specific, I could do that, too. The nurses always had questions for me, and I would try my best to answer them. Sometimes, they would mix a letter or two up and that would force me to re-spell things. That was both frustrating and comical at the same time. I would often think "this is the silliest way to communicate I've ever seen," but it worked. I couldn't write things on paper, because I was lying flat and couldn't see the paper easily. It was easier to feel the letters in your palm than it was to decipher my chicken scratch on paper. I recall one "rule of combat" I learned in the military, "If it's stupid and it works, it's not stupid." That's how I felt about my palm writing.

From my cardiac arrest, I acquired skin burns from the defibrillator paddles and a bruise where a machine called an "autopulse" was used to give me CPR. The autopulse was a system they strap to your chest and it provides chest compressions during the code. In spite of the bruise, I was thankful they used it. I had no chest muscles to speak of. I looked very much like a concentration camp survivor. If a real person tried doing chest compressions on me, I'm afraid they might have fractured my ribs or even my sternum. The autopulse worked great for me.

But I knew that my body took a beating from the code blue nonetheless. I didn't really want to go through that again. So, in the best palm writing I could muster, I informed Karen, Kora, Harvey, and Amy, my nurse, that I wanted to be a DNR or "Do Not Resuscitate" patient. Karen was very surprised at my decision and her and Kora had a small cry over it. But I knew that if the Lord chose to take me again, I did not want anybody intervening. Plus that, I wasn't sure what more my body could take in my present condition. So Amy got the forms organized and Karen signed it as my POA (Power of Attorney).

While I was on the ventilator, several people came to visit. My pastor and a few elders came by, and later in the week some close friends also stopped by. I would write in their hands or listen to Karen talk about things with them if I was too tired to interact.

When alone with Karen, I tried to address what I thought was pressing bill issues. In trying to cut down our monthly costs, I wanted to drop some of the items on our cell phone plan. Our company required that it be done at the end of a pay period. That day turned out to be the day after my cardiac arrest. I remember explaining who to call and our password information to Karen through palm writing and telling her she needed to make the call so we could start saving money. They looked at me as if I were nuts. I mean, I go through all of this, and my big issue is a phone bill? Now that I think about it, I probably was a little nuts.

CHAPTER FIFTEEN

Back from the Dead

They had tried to wean me off the ventilator a few times before, without success. They talked about giving me a tracheotomy, but they would try getting me off the ventilator one more time before that. So, after 5 days on the ventilator, my pulmonologist Dr. Harmon, decided to give it one more try. Though I've seen thousands of people get extubated after their operations, this whole process was a new experience for me. But I was willing. So without fanfare, they cut down the ventilator support and my lungs began to respond. Not a lot, but enough to consider it all a good sign. They then removed my endotracheal tube. I had a mild sore throat initially, and it was difficult for me to breathe due to being so very weak.

They quickly put me on a bipap machine. This provided me with positive pressure breathing through a mask instead of a tube. The mask was secured to my head with straps. This was very similar to the way pilots breathe with their masks. They also kept me on high flow oxygen to make every breath count.

I had to sit up because I still had limited control of my throat and I was unable to cough. So anything that went down my throat like saliva risked going down "the wrong pipe" and becoming a problem for me. The other issue was that, with my endotracheal tube in me for 5 days, I hadn't eaten anything during that time. The only thing I took in since my arrest was fluids through my IV, so my strength was nothing.

It didn't take me long to realize that my body wasn't quite ready to breathe without thinking about it. I just knew that if I didn't concentrate on completing every breath, my body would stop breathing. And now that I was a DNR patient, there would be no code blue called if I arrested again. I considered changing my status, but I still believed my body wouldn't be able to take another code blue attempt. And I wasn't in the mood to do it again, anyway.

I remember Harvey being near the bed while I was processing all this. Through palm writing, I told him that I wasn't sure if I'd make it through the night. It all rested on my will to live. Not my strength, because I had none. Just dogged determination to live. I began to focus on a specific tile on the ceiling to help me concentrate on my breathing. Amy wanted to give me some sedation so I could rest, but I told her I needed to be awake. Karen thought I might like the TV on, but I requested no distractions. I focused on that ceiling tile for 2 days straight before I felt comfortable enough to sleep.

I'm amazed how God inspires us to keep going while on earth. When I died, I was ready for it. Now that I was going to live, I had to fight for it! I had to be devoted to it! I had to purposefully act on my desire to live! This was not going to be a passive process in the least.

Someone stayed with me each night to make sure things went well. Often it was Karen and/or one of my boys. If I needed anything, they were ready to help. When I acquired a fair amount of phlegm from the bipap machine, they would disconnect my mask for a minute and suction my throat out before replacing the mask. That was a frequent issue early on.

Marcus from respiratory therapy came by to check on

me. He listened to my lungs and asked me to cough. When I was unable, he offered to use a vest that vibrated my chest for me, allowing phlegm to collect and be more easily expressed. The process was unique. It felt like being in one of those 1950s machines that places a belt around your waist and then jostles it, thereby shaking you up. It almost bounced me out of the bed. When he was satisfied it had done its work, he stopped the vest and took it off. It got the phlegm off of my bronchi, but it made it difficult to breathe. Marcus then slid a small suction tube down my nose and into my bronchi to get the phlegm out. That was a very uncomfortable procedure, but it worked great. After, I felt much better. He also gave me nebulizer therapy four times each day.

The next day, Jill came in Marcus' place and did the same thing to me. The third night brought a newer technician. When she also offered a vibrating vest treatment, I took her up on it. After the treatment, she tried to get a suction into my lungs, but was unable. This put me in a bad spot. Now I had phlegm collected, but no way to get it out. Since it was late in the evening, she had no one available to fall back on, so she apologized and then left. That night was one of my most difficult breathing nights ever. Brian stayed with me that night and helped suction my mouth out every time anything came up.

In the morning, Marcus came by and suctioned what he could out of my lungs. Man, did I feel better after that! I told him I would no longer use the vest unless someone was present who could suction out my lungs. He agreed.

I had a friend stop by one day who I did not expect, Dr. John Millspaugh. He and I worked together when I was in the military, and we always got along well. He used to do the craziest things in clinic. He had a large fake tarantula that was sound sensitive. He rigged it up over our office door and whenever anyone administrative came by to discuss something, he'd pretend like he was looking for something in a drawer. When he closed the drawer, it would activate the tarantula and scare them silly as it popped down from above. He even made movie parodies with staff members doubling for the real movie characters. He was always thinking of ways to lighten the mood in the clinic.

Anyway, he and his wife showed up while I was in ICU. This was incredibly unexpected because he lives in Tennessee! I guess his family had been on vacation in California and he wanted to stop by on his way back home. He had been keeping up with my Facebook posts and knew my condition was serious. So I had been off the ventilator for just a few short days and was very weak. But I put on the best smile I could and tried to interact.

He had brought several muscle magazines to help inspire me to grow stronger. It was great to see him, though I didn't have much stamina available. I tried to talk but found that talking and trying to breathe at the same time was not working out for me. Karen filled them in for me once it was clear I was too tired to continue. I recall thinking how it would have been nicer for them to come after I healed a bit more and had better strength. It really didn't occur to me that folks were trying to see me before I die. I was just thinking it was nice that they came.

Having been without solid food for a week, they decided to place a nasogastric (or NG) tube through my nose and down into my stomach to provide me nutrition. They explained how the procedure would go, and then they proceeded to drive the NG tube down my nose. Though it wasn't the worst thing to happen to me by far, it was challenging, especially in my frail condition. I remember thinking, "You know, I could probably tolerate this a lot better if I was healthy." Of course, if I were healthy, I realized, I wouldn't need an NG tube.

Once the NG tube got into me, they began providing me with real nutrition. As the treatment started, I began to feel my stomach fill just a bit. Within a brief period of time from the first feeding, I could feel the strength coming back to me. It was like Popeye getting into a can of spinach. What a noticeable difference! I wanted to go conquer the world, or at least roll from side to side in my bed (comparable in my current condition). My eyes quickly brightened and I felt much more alert.

While still on the ventilator, they had taken out my leg IV. Now they removed my central line. As for my breathing, they also began decreasing the amount of oxygen I was on. I was beginning to feel like I was on the mend. Though I still could not move anywhere, my body was slowly coming back.

As for bowel movements, I could never tell when it was time, so they placed chux pads under me and I went to the bathroom in my bed. Then, when I was done, I would notify them and they would roll me from side to side, clean me up, and get me back in place. Modesty was definitely a thing of the past. I met many staff members for the first time when they came to clean me up.

Dr. Washington came to visit and, after reassessing me, stated that he'd like to put me on a drug called Cyclophosphamide. This was a medication that could be given orally or through the NG tube to help suppress my immune system. Now usually I was pretty open to any different medication he wanted to try. But since I had a terrible experience with Rituximab, which had a pharmaceutical trade name that sounded similar to Cyclophosphamide's trade name, I was a bit leery to consider it. But he assured me the two drugs were not related, so I agreed to the trial.

So, later that day two chemo nurses came in to administer the Cyclophosphamide. They came into the room and put-on special gowns, gloves, and masks. Then they draped my NG tube and prepped everything for administration. They told me this is a well-tolerated medication and should give me no significant problems. I had to laugh, looking at them in full dress regalia, telling me there's no risk with the medication. "If I was already anxious about this, your outfits wouldn't relieve my fears," I said with a smirk.

Well, they gave me my dose, and amazingly enough, nothing untoward happened. I tolerated the medicine well and it seemed to be doing good for my condition. I was just happy my breathing wasn't affected by it. The chemo nurses then became daily visitors to my room.

The bipap mask soon started rubbing my nose bridge raw. In no time at all, I had a large scab developing on it. I couldn't come off the positive pressure support, so they had to start adjusting the mask to diminish the skin damage. That helped some.

Though urination was taken care of by my catheter, bowel movements and towel baths occurred in the bed due to my limited mobility. Chux were always under me in case "the need" arose. I wish I could use the bedside commode but getting me into one was just too cumbersome. I tried a bed pan once, but without any gluteus (butt cheek) muscles, it was a very sore experience for me. And still unable to void on command, it also was unsuccessful.

Movement required a team effort. If I wanted to get into my wheelchair, several techs came in and, using a ceiling lift system, guided me to the wheelchair and then set pillows about me to diminish pressure points. Then they would place oxygen on me, put suction around me, and put the nurse call button within easy reach. In the wheelchair, I would be able to use the arm rests and get my hands high enough to feed myself. This helped inspire me to try and be more independent.

Breathing was also better in the wheelchair. My pulmonologist told me that "the body is designed to breathe in an upright position. Breathing while in bed (even when the bed is upright) is more difficult on the body." The more I could stay upright, the better my breathing would be. That gave me a new-found reason to get up in the morning and get out of bed.

Me before my diagnosis

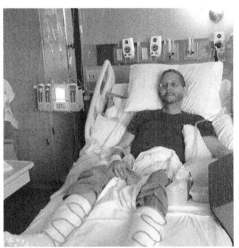

Me shortly before I coded

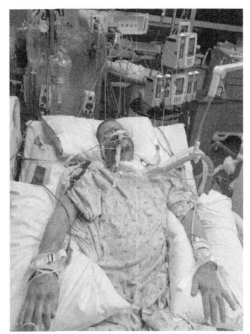

Me after I coded

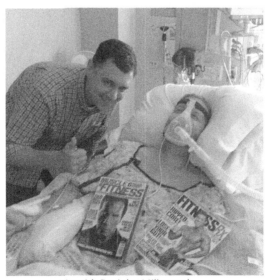

Me with Dr. John Millspaugh

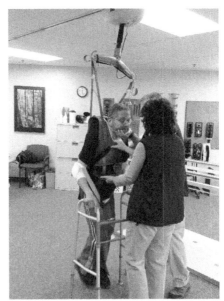

PT during second hospitalization

Me with my beautiful wife, Karen

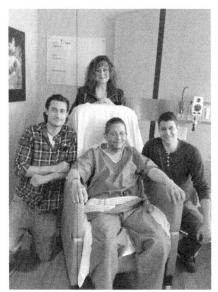

Me with Karen and our boys

Me with my brothers

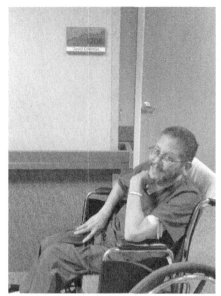

Me outside the Rehab room

Me outside the nursing home

CHAPTER SIXTEEN

What You Can Affect

I remember reading a book by ex-Navy Seal Mark Owen called "No Hero." It spoke about him getting caught on a mountainside during rock climbing training and having a panic attack. He had a fear of heights, and all of a sudden his fear took over and he was unable to move. Though he had come a long way from ground level, he still had about 150 feet left before he reached the top. He just froze in place and couldn't move.

Then one of the real rock climbers, thin and lanky, crawled up alongside him without any rope support whatsoever. He casually said, "Hey, man, just stay in your three-foot world." "My what?," Mark shot back. "Your three-foot world. What's above and below you doesn't matter. Focus only on what you can affect, what is within your reach. Where will you place your right hand. Then your left hand. Then your right foot, and then your left foot. Nothing else matters except for that."

Using that logic helped him overcome his fear and complete his task. He said later that he used the "three-foot world" strategy during missions when things were challenging and getting complicated. He would just focus on the immediate task until it was completed.

I used the same strategy each day I was in the hospital. Though things were happening at home and issues would arise daily from the US mail (bills, correspondence), I focused on what it would take to move myself in bed. How could I get into a side position and still breathe comfortably? How do I get my hand onto the side bar and hold the position? By focusing on my "three-foot world," it helped me simplify my activities and move easier. I even found a Biblical verse that relates to the "three-foot world" concept. It's Matthew 6:31-34. The last verse stating, "So do not worry about tomorrow, for tomorrow will take care of itself. Each day has enough trouble of its own."

I gradually improved my breathing to the point that positive pressure breathing no longer became a necessity. They moved me to oxygen via nasal cannula. I was still on high flow oxygen, but without the bipap mask, was able to let my nasal bridge heal.

Rebuilding my arms was a very slow process. Since I had no real pecs or biceps to speak of, lifting weights was just not an option for me. So occupational therapy started out by giving me a foam ball and having me hold it with my fingers while pushing my hands together. Where the average individual could easily compress the ball that way, I had the hardest time getting it to just slightly compress. They also tied elastic bands to my wheelchair, and I would grab them and try to move my arm through several range-of-motion exercises with the bands acting as resistance. Again, we had to start with the thinnest bands otherwise I couldn't get my arms to move at all.

When my wife was at the hospital, she would often feed me so I wouldn't make a mess during my meals. Then one day, she had to leave before dinner arrived. I mentioned my dining concerns to her, and she said, "Well, try feeding yourself and see how it goes." It struck me as funny that I hadn't thought about doing that myself. Since I had been working with PT and OT for several days and had been getting stronger incrementally every day, it didn't occur to me that I would be strong enough to attempt new tasks now. So, when dinner came, I had the staff position everything within my reach and, taking my time, I carefully began to feed myself. I wouldn't have been able to do it in bed but using the arm rests on the wheelchair to keep my arms high enough, I could reach my mouth with a fork and get through my meal just fine. A straw in my drink glass helped me with fluid intake, as I still didn't have enough strength to hold a drink glass with any great coordination. But after dinner, I was feeling quite proud of my recent accomplishment.

After that, I always tried to feed myself. Since I was still only allowed soft foods, for breakfast I would get eggs over easy so they would have a consistency more favorable to my swallowing abilities. I would have the cafeteria place the eggs in a bowl to allow me better control of my food and less risk of spillage. Oatmeal also went down well, so that too became a standard request for each morning. Fruit did well for me, so I also took that when offered.

Lunch and dinner often consisted of chicken noodle soup or other easily digestible fare. I was hesitant to try harder foods since swallowing had given me problems previously. But as my muscles began to return, speech/swallow therapy rechecked my abilities, and found I could start eating more solid foods without a problem. This was a pleasant surprise for me. I had been watching TV commercials about "mouthwatering" foods like pizza, burgers, or anything solid. I would think, "Man, I wish I could eat that." But I knew it was not meant to be. Now I was cleared to try whatever I desired.

The evening I got my food clearance, I ordered a burger from the cafeteria. All I could think about was all of those burger commercials from fast food joints to sit down restaurants showing juicy full-bodied offerings ready to please the most discerning pallet. When my burger arrived, it looked like something someone found in the back of the freezer and decided to microwave it just to put it out of its misery. It bore no resemblance to anything remotely identified as a burger on TV, but there it was, nonetheless.

So, with all the gusto of a man who hadn't eaten solid food for over three ½ months, I bit into it hoping the flavor would be better than the presentation. If I had closed my eyes, it would have been difficult to tell whether I had placed food or softened shoe leather in my mouth. As far as burgers go, it was a poor excuse for one. But I ate it all because it was my first one in a long time, and I was not going to give up on a challenge. I was able to swallow each bite without physical difficulty, which was a pleasant revelation. You'll be happy to know I survived both my hospital stay and that burger!

CHAPTER SEVENTEEN

My Other Challenges

My blood sugar throughout my hospital stay would not stabilize due to the considerable amount of steroids I was on. Though my food intake was fairly routine and primarily meat and vegetable focused, my blood sugar would be anywhere from normal to the high 300s. Whenever it was high, I would look at them and say, "I'm only eating what you all give me. It's not like the ice cream truck stops by my room for a visit while you're gone."

Regulating my diabetes required a great deal more injections as an in-patient than I routinely gave myself at home. Finger sticks and insulin injections were frequent happenings throughout my day. Though I wasn't used to having injections before my illness, I eventually didn't even flinch. Needles no longer held any real threat to me.

I continued to gain strength daily, though sometimes I was the only one to notice. It might come in the fact I could roll from side to side easier today than I did yesterday. Or when PT evaluated me, I was able to stand by locking my knees a few seconds longer than I could the day before. With OT, I noticed I was gradually able to reach farther up the side of my head than before. And my swallowing continued to improve to the point where I almost didn't have to think about swallowing, it just came naturally.

I still didn't have the ability to cough with any force. Clearing my throat "with enthusiasm" was getting better, but that was about all I could muster. They gave me respiratory tools to aid in lung improvement, such as pipe with a ball which moved when one exhaled into the mouthpiece at the bottom of the pipe. The object of the contraption was to keep the ball in a certain range as long as possible. Everything that appeared simple to most always challenged my current abilities.

CHAPTER EIGHTEEN

Moving On Up

They decided to move me from the "progressive ICU" to the third floor. The move would require a few assistants since I still had IV tubes, oxygen requirements, suction needs, and a foley catheter to contend with. The plan was to move me in my bed to the elevator and take that up one floor to my new room. I had improved my breathing well enough to where they felt I could move without oxygen support, and I agreed.

After dinner, they untangled me from all of my wall attachments, disconnected my oxygen, and we began our journey. I was doing well enough to comment to all the staff I passed, "Hey, look at me. No oxygen." They smiled as I went by along with my parade of medical paraphernalia. It was good to break free even for only a brief period.

Once I got to the third floor and into my room, they began hooking me back up to all of the monitors and wall supports. Oxygen was placed back on me, but at a very low dose. Again, I survived without any significant pain in my body. Each transition to a new location made me feel a little bit better about my improvements. It was another sign of my continued, yet ever so slight, positive change in health.

Later that evening, I was visited by the chief nurse of the hospital and some of her staff. They informed me they might have to send me back to progressive ICU. "Do I have a health change I don't know about," I asked? "No," they replied. It was because I had signed a limited

DNR order. Though they could manage that issue on the second floor, they didn't allow those orders on any of the other floors. "So," I said, "what you're telling me is that you consider your floor nurses substandard to your ICU nurses for being able to make a decision on DNR orders?" "No. They are all quality nurses. It's just hospital policy." "Oh. So you have a hospital policy that penalizes your RNs based on their work location, and not on their abilities. Is that what I'm hearing?" They then talked it over with the floor RN staff and agreed to leave me on the floor. That worked for me.

CHAPTER NINETEEN

One Step Closer to Normal

Though still wheelchair bound, they began discussing when they might transition me to a rehab facility to continue my healing. Debra, from the transition office, came by and described the facilities in the surrounding area able to take me on. Most rehab facilities were extensions of nursing homes. It was very surreal discussing which "nursing home" I'd like to transition to at my age. I always figured this issue wouldn't come up until I was old and grey. Well, I was indeed greying and "old" was a relative term, but still it came as a mild shock to be seriously talking about this now.

The home with the latest equipment was recently built and, because of that, was yet to be approved by my insurance to send me there. The next newest facility was a little over 1 year old and was also one town north of me. That one was on the list of eligible rehab locations. It was also an easy drive from the freeway, so I decided on it. Debra said she would submit the paperwork and would know of the insurance decision by the next day.

It was weird talking about leaving the hospital, since I hadn't been out for over 2 months. When I arrived for my first admission, it was springtime. Now it was well into the summer. My mind was having a tough time adjusting without frequent outside stimulus to verify the change. I was getting into a routine as a long-time hospital patient. Though uncomfortable at first, it was now becoming "normal" for me. Breaking free from it would be a bit unnerving. Now that I think about it, it's amazing how fast we get ourselves into a habit we don't want to leave.

CHAPTER TWENTY

Praising God in All Things

I recall having a dream one night where I woke up in my bed at my home, normal and able to function. I woke my wife up and said, "Honey, did I ever have the wildest dream. I dreamed I couldn't walk, and all my muscles wasted away, and then I wound up in the hospital and had to endure many tests and experimental therapies. And I needed help to do everything from going to the bathroom, to showering, to feeding myself, and to getting around. It was the most vivid dream I ever had." I was staring at how easily I could walk around and do normal things.

I was taking it all in, when suddenly I awoke in my hospital bed with my legs padded and still unable to move. Nurses were milling about out in the hall, and I realized that whole dream was itself a dream. I was still going to have to work on improving my muscle structure the hard way, day by day through physical and occupational therapy and by proper dietary habits.

Finding myself back in the hospital bed and in my weak physical state again was one of the most challenging mental hurdles I had to overcome. You really want things to "go your way." I didn't want to have to endure anymore, since I felt I had endured enough already. But I had to remind myself that this wasn't about me. It was about God and His plans for me. It was about changes I was going through and people who were experiencing God through me and my condition. It was about me being willing to suffer a few "unpleasantries" if

God desired it.

Every morning, I would wake up and pray the same basic prayer, "Lord, if you would heal me right now from this condition, I'll go through the hospital ward dancing and singing Your praises. But if Your will is that I continue in this illness, please give me the strength I need to face today's challenges and help me continue to praise You through this and be a light for You in this condition."

Since I was eating well, they decided to remove my NG tube. The other option if I required it longer would be to have a tube surgically placed through my abdomen directly into my stomach for long-term feeding. I recall discussing this further with the hospitalist. I may have been eating better, but having food placed through the tube at night was a terrific way for me to get my needed protein and vegetables into my system. I was having a challenging time eating a similar volume of food during the day.

"You know Dave, the surgery carries risks and having a long-term feeding tube also carries risks," Dr. Desmond said. "I know, but it's nice to augment my meals easily at night." "Dave, I really don't recommend this since you're on immuno-suppressants and you're still weak." "Oh, all right," I conceded. "I'll just keep increasing my diet and getting my nutrition through my food intake...like everyone else on the planet." I could hear how silly my argument was. Everyone else gets their nutrition from their food intake. My body is set up for things to happen naturally. I just wanted to take an easier approach to the problem. To consider surgery an "easier approach" from just taking in an oral diet sounds crazy to me now, but that was my thought process back then.

So, the next day, they removed the NG tube, a much

nicer process than putting one in, I might add. They also removed my foley catheter since I was slowly getting better use of my arms and could hold a urinal for myself when I needed to go. I also had gotten better at determining when I needed to have a bowel movement. Because of my diminished gluteus muscles, it always felt hard and uncomfortable to use the bedpan, but they could hoist me onto the toilet or to a bedside commode for a bowel movement. I still couldn't wipe myself but allowing me to do what I could gave me just a little better feeling of independence.

CHAPTER TWENTY-ONE

Rehab or Bust

Well, on June 17th, I was finally cleared to move to a fairly modern rehab facility in Northern Colorado. They placed me in a wheelchair and transported me by van to the rehab center. Karen and the boys followed behind in their cars. It was funny being alone in the back of a moving van, wheelchair strapped to the floor, and me without much neck muscles to speak of. I placed my arms on the wheelchair rests and put my hands on both sides of my jaw to keep my head in place. It made me look comfortable without giving away the nervous feeling I had about keeping my head up. We did arrive safely, but I could feel every turn and breaking move we made.

It was a two-story facility that held the nursing home on the second floor and the rehab unit on the first floor. It was late in the afternoon when we arrived, and they brought me right over to my room. It was one of several they had with a Hoyer lift system built right into the ceiling. They slid the Hoyer pad underneath me and attached me to the lift. Then, with the press of a button, up I went into the air. No one had to "put their back" into lifting me (though they rarely had to do that even when they lifted me by hand). All they had to do was guide my body while it was moving so as not to bang my head along the way. Once I was over my bed, the lift brought me gently down onto the mattress. It was very cool! Then they took the pad out from under me and got me ready for dinner.

Eric was my nurse for the evening. He introduced me

to some of the night staff and explained the routines at the facility. "Here's the call bell. If you ring it, please allow 30-45 minutes for us to answer. We have limited staff here, so it takes a while for us to get to everybody." "...30-45 minutes," I thought. Wow, I'm used to 30-60 seconds on the hospital floors. But this is a non-critical environment and so things move a bit slower here. I'll just have to adjust to the new routine. I could tell my wife didn't like such a delay on response time, but we talked about it later and she felt better about it.

Dinner consisted of chicken fried steak and mashed potatoes. I was glad I had improved my swallowing enough to where I could eat almost anything in front of me. And I was thankful I had been feeding myself, since I don't think they would have the staff available to feed me if I needed it. I wasn't on oxygen anymore and was glad for that, too. I could ask for minimal staff support and would do OK throughout the rest of the day alone. This situation, I thought, would work out just fine.

After dinner, they got me back on the lift and took me over to the toilet. The system allowed me to be placed in a sitting position over the toilet and had a hole for me to "do my business through." Then they would hoist me up, wipe me off, and take me back to bed. Once in bed, they would put a tray table over my bed and place things on it that I needed, such as my urinal, a water bottle, and the remote control for my TV. The light switch for my room was at the head of the bed but had a chain switch that extended to the middle of my bed. If they clipped it to the middle, I could reach it when I needed to use the urinal without having to call someone in first. I would then lower my bed to make room for the urinal under the tray table. I would place a sheet over me in case anyone came in, and I would pee into the urinal. If I only urinated a small-medium amount, I would go back to bed and use it on my next void before calling someone in to empty it. That worked for the staff because they could get in and out of my room quickly. They often told me I wasn't much of a problem for them during the night.

Karen tried to stay each night until I was settled in after dinner. Once in bed, I didn't require much help at all. She usually came late morning or early afternoon. She would fill me in on what was going on at home, and I would give her info on my progress with my exercises and other happenings at the nursing home. It was nice having her come around. It kept me connected to her and a life outside of my current four walls. Having other guests drop by was also a treat. Marshall came by every 1-2 weeks to check up on me. We'd just shoot the breeze, but the mental stimulation was refreshing.

CHAPTER TWENTY-TWO

Learning the Rehab Ropes

My first morning in Rehab, several visitors came by. The nutritionist came over to discuss any diet issues I wanted addressed. I informed her my blood sugars were still all over the place due to my continued steroid intake. She said she would keep me on a diabetic diet to help with that. I also told her I wanted to grow muscles, so I needed a focused diet for that. She not only worked out a healthy meal plan but gave me a few protein bars to place on my tray, in case I had a low sugar, and no food was available. That was very thoughtful. She offered me the option of dining with other residents in the dining hall. I told her that since I was on immuno-suppressants, and most of the residents here were old and infirmed, I thought it would be best if I took my meals in my room to decrease my risk of acquiring a secondary infection. She understood.

Sheila, from Occupational Therapy, came by and did a full OT exam on me to assess the current status of my shoulder and hand muscles, and to determine a good course of treatment for me at the facility. I told her my biggest concern was my shoulders. She did a full evaluation on my upper extremities and then gave me a quick shoulder manipulation. She was tough, but firm. I felt better after she was done.

Andrea, from Physical Therapy, was next to arrive. She came in half-way through Sheila's eval, so they both worked on me at the same time for a while. Andrea did a full eval on my legs and also did range-of-motion exercises to keep things limber. While the two of them were together, it made it a bit difficult for me since I was trying to concentrate on the one who was talking to me, while the other working on me would ask a few questions of her own. I told them I felt like I was on a date with two women, trying to show focused attention to each and accomplishing it for neither. They laughed and promised they would only devote individual time to me in the future.

Ramona, from the admin side of the house, came by to tell me about evaluation issues and other routine happenings in rehab. They would be checking on my progress each week and would hold a formal board meeting on me in about 3 weeks. At that time, they would brief me on their findings and set goals for my graduation out of rehab. Considering I couldn't get out of anything they put me into (bed, wheelchair), it seemed a bit premature to hope for making it out of the facility any time soon.

But I was determined to try my best to make my stay here as short as possible. I started to focus on what was required to get me out of a wheelchair. "Let's see," I thought. "In order to get into a standing position, I need to have legs strong enough to push my body up, and I need arms strong enough to push up from the arm rests and assist my legs. It's a team effort."

At present, I didn't have enough arm or leg strength to even shift my bottom in my seat. If my butt got sore and I needed a change of position, I would have to ask a technician or one of my family members to get behind me and hoist me up from my arm pits. This was actually a relatively easy task for anyone, considering I only weighed about 130 lbs. It also made it more embarrassing for me, since I didn't even have the strength to shift 130 lbs. in a wheelchair seat. You could easily touch thumbs and index fingers together around my thighs. And my arms looked like they were without a stitch of muscle on them. I was still very different from the 180 lbs. I used to be before all of this started in April.

So I figured I needed to grow muscles in order to achieve my goal. I never thought about it before, but I specifically needed thigh muscles and pecs to make it all work. "So, how does one grow muscles?" Body builders came to mind. "OK, what do they do to grow muscles?" Well, they eat protein and vegetables, so that's what I would focus on. How do they grow specific muscles? Well, they eat right and exercise the muscles they wish to affect. OK then, I had the start of a plan. If I can grow these particular muscles, I might be able to hoist myself out of this wheelchair and get out of the nursing home.

I told Andrea and Sheila my goals and had them focus on building those muscles in me. They were agreeable to my requests and got right to work with an appropriate exercise program. I must admit, to work in PT or OT requires a significant amount of patience. I started out using foam objects to push in on, and elastic bands to move against, because no real weights were light enough for me to initially manage. 1 lb. weights felt quite heavy early on.

As for my legs, Andrea initially had me just lifting them from a supine position and also moving them laterally while they were just above the mattress pad. That felt almost herculean to perform. To help me move my leg laterally, sometimes she would put a waxed board under my heel. I would also need to have socks on, because my skin would cause enough friction on the board that it would stop my leg from moving. Boy, did I ever feel like a wimp!

I forced myself to focus on the goal and not the present results. Looking at my daily achievements were disheartening. But staying focused on the goal of eventually getting out of the chair, got me more determined. As my dad used to say, "The best way to eat an elephant... is one bite at a time." I found myself saying that often when coming up against various obstacles.

Every day time was allotted for me to work with PT and OT. Andrea would always get there at 8 am and take me down to the PT room. It had a large flat padded table that was adjustable in height and head incline. At first, when I was still very weak, she would push me over in my wheelchair. Then her and an aid would get me onto the table, and she would have me lift and move my legs. At first, no resistance was needed to make it hard for me. Anything above wiggling my toes was challenging for me.

After she had me move my legs, she began range-of-motion (ROM) exercises, where she would move my hips, knees, and ankles and occasionally have me hold a position until I fatigued. Then she would sit me up along the side of the table and use my legs to balance in my position. She also would get me up and have me lock my knees to remain standing. All of these tasks seem so trivial now but required a great deal of focus each day to accomplish. When you talk to your body and it doesn't respond, it's a very odd experience.

Sheila was just as brutal. She would have me push the wheelchair myself as far as I could go before helping me along. Once back to the PT room, she would sit me on the side of the table and put a large beach ball in between us. She would be sitting on a stool with rollers. Then she would have me push the ball (using only my arms – no body weight allowed) as hard as I could to try and move her and her stool backwards. No matter how hard I tried, early on she didn't move at all. And bear in mind, she probably weighed no more than 120 lbs. soaking wet. I felt like I just competed in an Olympic event. It was a very large effort on my part, and she didn't really budge at all! I was amazed.

She also took me through my arm ROMs and did some weightlifting activities, very little weight, I might add. She then tried her best to get me moving my arms in all directions unaided. It was a bit like being a newborn all over again. Movement without adequate muscle was very difficult to achieve. Even if she moved my arm to an endpoint of a position and had me hold it there by myself, I was rarely successful in that task.

Because my shoulder motions were limited, I always worried about adhesive capsulitis, or "frozen shoulder" as it's commonly referred. I felt that if I didn't pay attention to keeping my shoulders mobile, they would eventually scar down and require surgery to regain mobility. Sheila shared my concern and because of that, would take time each week to massage my shoulders and "take them through their paces."

I remember one day lying supine on the table and she got above me and put a hand on each shoulder. Then, using her weight, she forced my shoulders back and held the position for a while. It was a bit sore to do, but I always felt better afterwards. "Are you sure this isn't going to dislocate my shoulders," I'd often ask during our sessions? "Yes," she'd calmly reply. "You'll do fine." I'm happy to report that, in spite of what I felt was her best efforts to the contrary, my shoulders did indeed remain intact.

PT and OT worked me very hard relatively speaking. I

would get back to my room after their workouts, and sleep for a few hours just to recuperate. At first, my sessions required a great deal of effort on their part. They would often use an additional technician to help move me from my wheelchair to the table and back again. Sometimes, the technician would have to get behind me while I sat on the table, just to keep me upright. They would cheer me on, though I was merely a bit player in the whole affair. I just didn't have enough muscle to move myself with any authority.

But after a week or so, I began to do things just a bit better than before. Whereas before I could barely provide enough pressure on a foam ball between my hands to alter its shape, now I was actually holding and moving 1 lb. hand weights on command. Granted, I didn't move them much, but I could do some activities with them.

I continued reading my Bible every morning and taking time to pray. I found that the more I kept God close to me, the more He was close to me. One day, unexpectedly, a nurse mentioned to me, "You know we're all talking about you." "Really," I replied? "Yes. You're quite inspirational." I almost laughed aloud. "Me? You've got to be kidding me. I'm stuck in this bed. The proverbial bump on a log! You have to help me move from place to place and even wipe me up after I've gone to the bathroom. How in the world is that inspirational?" "Well, you're suffering through some extreme issues and yet we always see you smiling and cheerful," she began. "And it's easy to sense an overwhelming peace about you." "You're quite different."

I was stunned! Though I was unable to do anything (and I mean ANYTHING) of significance, God was still using me (in spite of my shortcomings) to show Himself to others around me! And she was not the only one to "stop by" and chat. Others came by and allowed me to share a bit of my faith and how I viewed God through all of my present trials. That built my spiritual strength immensely.

CHAPTER TWENTY-THREE

The Occasional Outing

Another treatment they continued while I was in the rehab facility, was IgG treatments. This consisted of me going by bus to the local hospital and spending a few hours at the outpatient infusion clinic. This clinic had several beds and reclining chairs to allow patients to be comfortable while staff administered medication through an IV. We all had TV sets in our pods and could watch a show while receiving our treatments. The most common treatment there was chemotherapy for cancer. My disease wasn't cancer, but many treatments given to me were also used in cancer therapy, though I didn't go through hair loss or any untoward side effects.

I started out coming to them in a wheelchair and having to be transferred to one of their bed units. This allowed me to elevate my head and place a bend in the bed for my knees. I would also place a urinal between my legs under the sheets so I could discreetly use it without having to be taken to the bathroom

IgG therapy helped build up protein in my body and gave me tools to rebuild my muscles from a devastating disease. At first, right after I arrived, they would take my vital signs (blood pressure, pulse, weight) and then give me acetaminophen and diphenhydramine as a preparatory measure. Then they would start an IV. Sometimes they would find a vein right away. Other times it would require a few "sticks" to get things secure.

I used to like coming to the infusion clinic, because it was a day out of the nursing home, and they would serve food from the hospital cafeteria. My personal favorite was chicken strips and fries. It provided additional protein and it wasn't often served at the nursing home. That coupled with a few hours to myself to enjoy a show or a movie, was quite relaxing. Because of the effects my body had to endure receiving the IgG, they didn't want me doing much on the days I had my therapy. I was OK with that since I was usually very tired when I returned.

Over time, I became strong enough to transfer from the wheelchair almost unaided, so I began using the reclining chairs instead of the bed. The infusion clinic staff would look at me curiously each time I arrived, because I got better month to month and eventually (after being discharged from the nursing home) transferred myself unaided to the recliners. They were not used to seeing someone recover so quickly.

CHAPTER TWENTY-FOUR

Settling In

Staff changed throughout the week and also at night. Being there as long as I was, I got to know the staff fairly well. The nurses were very helpful. Whenever I had a request, they tried their best to accommodate me. I kept my requests as limited as possible. Once I was in bed for the night, I usually only needed someone to empty my urinal from time to time.

In the morning, I would have them get me out of bed and into my wheelchair. That provided me with some degree of mobility. Though I couldn't get up from the chair (or move my bottom at all, for that matter), I could roll to the mayo stand bedside table for eating. If I was careful, I didn't spill anything, so no further assistance was required.

Trying to keep from acquiring a local respiratory infection, I stayed in my room as much as possible. The door remained open, so I got to watch residents as they passed by. Some were ambulatory, getting about unaided. Most were in wheelchairs or walkers. They would all either be walking the hallways for exercise or heading off to the dining area or a scheduled meeting with a therapist. As I watched them, I'm sure they watched me as they filed past my door. I must have looked pretty boring, always sitting in my wheelchair in my room. But it's amazing what will pass for entertainment when you're living in a nursing home.

I usually had access to the TV remote control, so I was free to browse as many channels as were available to me, which as I recall, was somewhere around thirty channels. A few were Spanish channels, and some were soap channels. I found my favorite ten channels and often stayed with them to find my entertainment. In spite of the number of channels I had, often there was no good show on TV. I joked a few times that though I possessed no functional use of Spanish, I watched the Spanish channel on occasion just to break up the monotony of the other offerings.

Twice a week, we'd get baths. This was one of those things I just had to allow to be done with assistance. I no longer had the ability to be in a shower situation by myself safely. And even if I could get in there by myself, I still had no reach to cover my whole body. No matter how independent I used to be, I no longer could take a shower without significant help. But when you need help to get a job done, modesty becomes the least of your worries. If the staff member is unphased by the activity and is polite and helpful, it's easy to accept the support.

Heather was a lady in her forties. She had been working at the nursing home for many years. She made the whole thing seem matter of fact. She laid out several towels, got soap and shampoo items ready, and started the shower so it would be warm when I got in. Then she got me out of my old clothes and wheeled me into the shower bay. She would then help me get onto a shower seat and would wash me on the shower seat. The shower extension handle made it easy to direct water to wherever it was needed. Since I had the ability to reach my abdomen and groin, she would lather up a hand towel and give it to me for cleaning those areas. She would concentrate her efforts on my back, face, hair, and legs. Just feeling hot shower water run over my body was refreshing. Even though I couldn't do it alone, it still made me feel a bit more human and normal.

After we were done, she would give me another towel to dry off the areas I could reach, and she began drying off the other areas. Once that was done, she would get me back into an adult diaper (a precautionary measure only) and help me back into my wheelchair. Then she would get me into fresh pajamas, and make sure I was ready for the rest of my day. I thought it would be an awkward endeavor, but she made it very relaxing and natural. After everything else I had been through, modesty took a back seat to necessity.

Bowel movements also required help. I'd have to call the medical assistant in to help transfer me onto the toilet. They used the ceiling Hoyer lift machine to get me to the toilet. Once there, they would lower me onto the seat and I would remain attached to the ceiling. That helped me maintain my position without worry of falling off the toilet. I had also lost abdominal muscles in my condition, so I didn't have the normal support when I went to push stool out. Any resistance whatsoever to stool moving (such as constipation and a sphincter muscle at the end of it all) would be too great an obstacle to overcome since my abdominal muscles were marginal in strength. What worked for me was if someone placed a gait belt on my lower abdomen. Then I could push against the belt and the bowel movement would happen more easily.

Oral medications also created challenges. Prior to my diagnosis, I had very few pills that I took. One diabetic medication, one anti-hypertensive, and one cholesterol lowering medication daily. After I was diagnosed with Dermatomyositis, I was on IV steroids during my hospital stay, but that changed over to oral steroids during my time in rehab. I was also on Cyclophosphamide for immuno-suppression, Folic Acid, docusate sodium to keep me from getting constipated again, and losartan for blood pressure. I was also on a chronic antibiotic to keep me from getting an unexpected infection from the Cyclophosphamide. Throughout my hospital and nursing home stays, I remained on IV IG once a month and on insulin daily based on my current blood glucose levels.

The oral medications required a little routine to get it down. Since my swallowing had only recently begun to improve, I did best taking my medication with something soft, such as oatmeal or yogurt. I would put a wad of the food in my mouth, and then take the pills and insert them in the wad with my tongue. This allowed me to take several small pills at one time very easily. For larger pills, I would insert them into their own wad of soft food and swallow them one at a time. Taking medicine with drinks never seemed to work as well for me. It wouldn't bind together like soft food would and so sometimes it would go down with the drink swallow, sometimes not.

Some nurses understood my plight and would provide me with a full container of yogurt. Occasionally, I would get someone who would put a dollop or two of yogurt into a small paper medicine cup and give it to me. It hardly had enough yogurt to go over a few of the pills, let alone everything I had to take. I always felt bad asking for something and it was challenging having them give it to me in an unexpected way. I would then try my best to make it work anyway, just to keep them from having to redo my request.

Some nurses tried to make things a bit more bearable for me. Because of my small frame, they were always trying to keep a good calorie intake going in me. I used to supplement my diet with ensure. Tasting a bit like gritty chocolate milk, it wasn't the best tasting treat around, but it got calories into me just fine. Eric was an evening nurse who used to put my night ensure in a glass with frozen yogurt or ice cream to help me gain weight and to improve the taste. It wasn't something you'd serve at a 5-star restaurant, but to me, it was my own small slice of heaven. It's amazing what a little kindness will do for one's morale. I felt like a king sitting in bed, watching a show, and sipping on my ensure smoothie. Life, in spite of its obvious shortcomings, was good during those times.

Small blessings were found daily around every corner. My morning meal was served to me in separate bowls because it was easier for me to use bowls to feed myself than to use a plate when dealing with soft foods. I ordered the same meal every morning because I could swallow it without much difficulty, poached eggs, oatmeal, some fruit, and yogurt. Milk was the preferred drink because I wanted to insure adequate calcium in my diet. It got so routine, the cooks just sent my meal to me in bowls without me even asking for it.

The nutrition director, Janet, would make sure I had a stock of instant breakfast bars at my bedside in case I felt hungry or had to get to PT before breakfast came. It was just the thing to augment my mealtimes.

The morning MA, Brenda, knew that I needed my TV remote, my tray table, my water jug filled, and my computer tablet within reach of my wheelchair after moving me from my bed. She would just go right to work putting everything in its place after getting me seated without so much as a word from me. Then before she left my room, she would say, "There, Mr. Coleman, I think I got everything for you. Is there anything else you need?"

"No, Brenda. I think you got it all. Thank you very much." They always tried to be there when I needed something without interrupting my privacy time.

When bedtime came (usually in the 7pm timeframe), the MAs would come in and get me situated with pillows under my elbows and everything within easy reach. My tray table was high enough so that when I needed to use the urinal, I could lower my bed and have room to do my business without additional MA support. After it filled up, I would ring my call bell and someone would come and empty it out and replace it for future use. They were all very helpful.

After they placed me in bed, I would watch TV or work on my computer until I wanted to go to sleep, which was usually around 11pm. But I required little from the staff while in bed so they were happy to get me in bed as soon as I desired. From that point on until morning, they knew right where to find me for blood draws, injections, or anything else required.

CHAPTER TWENTY-FIVE

The Rebuilding Begins

As time went on, I began to notice minor changes in my strength. I used to place the bed in a high head-up position in the morning. Even with that, I couldn't move in any direction without staff helping me to get my legs to a bedside and lifting my upper body into position. Gradually, I could initiate movement in my legs, though support was still required to finalize my desires. And over time, I began to roll my upper body to the bedside while staff worked my legs.

Movement in general for me seemed an odd thing. Though I wanted my body to move, nothing wanted to comply. My forearms and hands had limited mobility, but not a lot of strength or range of motion. My legs felt like dead weight every time I tried to get them going. If I wanted to shift my bottom in bed, I needed staff support to make it happen. Since I couldn't reach my head, pillow adjustments also required staff intervention to make it happen.

After about a week and a half at the rehab center, I had enough arm strength to push off of an upright bed to initiate movement. It wasn't enough, mind you, to get myself upright in bed, but it was enough to show promise. I also went from full Hoyer lift from the ceiling to a Sabina lift. It rolled about on the floor and once strapped in, would allow one person to lift you off of a bed, chair, or toilet and move you anywhere in the room. It did require you to be able to lock your legs and provide minimal support, but I felt much better moving in it vs.

having to use a larger lift machine.

Every day I went to the gym with PT and OT, I tried to get just a little bit better at the activities. While lying on the matted table, Sheila would try to get me to hold my arms above my head. Then she would put them at my side and have me move my arms above my head without assistance. Early on, that was a very difficult task to do. Sometimes she would provide resistance to my arm movements to help build my strength.

After a long workout, she would save time and massage my shoulders and arms to give my miniscule muscles a rest. I would often be amazed at how patient these PT and OT technicians were to people like me. I mean, the speed in which I was demonstrating improvement made glaciers look like river rapids! I ate my protein and vegetables, and I went to the rehab gym to assess whatever new muscle growth occurred. But Sheila and Andrea never seemed to be bothered watching me run through my exercises. They just had me do what I could over and over and over again. And they were happy for me when I accomplished it, and they worked with me when I didn't quite succeed in completing the task.

Andrea would have me go through range-of-motion activities with my legs. At first, it was just trying to improve my ability to move my legs. Then, she began to provide resistance to my movement. At the end of my sessions, she would take my legs through passive range-of-motion exercises and that always helped to relax my muscles better.

Both of them would try to have me sit up from a supine position and prepare myself to transfer to my wheelchair. It took a few weeks to build enough core muscles to make it work. At first, I relied a great deal on them to help me get up. But eventually, they helped a lot less and I did a bit more. When trying to stand from a seated position, I had neither the thigh strength nor the chest/arm strength to achieve it. But I knew that once those muscles grew and I could get out of a chair all by myself, I would be ready to leave the nursing home.

Having those two ladies work with me was inspirational. Many times I looked at the task before me and thought this was too great to accomplish in a reasonable amount of time. But they were patient and persistent. They'd focus my attention on each task and talk (and walk) me through every activity on my schedule for each day. They had sincere care for my condition and an ardent desire to help me succeed in my goals. And over time, I didn't want to let them down, so I always tried a little harder every day.

When I started to improve, changes were gradual at first. I remember being able to move my legs ever so slightly in the bed one night. Feet have always been easy to move, but legs were stationary. One night, I needed them a bit more apart than they already were, and I managed to move them just enough to get my urinal between my legs easily. I was quite pleased and surprised. Up until that point, I always had to call someone in to move my legs for me. It was the weirdest thing to have a body that didn't usually respond to my commands. Now, things were starting to come back.

When I showed the staff, they were impressed I had a change in movement, slight as it was. But I was hopeful. I kept on eating protein and vegetables and worked out with the staff every time I was scheduled. Andrea began to see some strength changes in my legs. Where once they didn't move, now I could send them in a given direction, as long as we made sure no friction was present. I slowly began to move my legs outward (abduction) and inward (adduction). They didn't go far, nor was it a smooth movement, but it was visible.

It's amazing what overcoming simple tasks can do for one's spirit. The activities were relatively hard for a weakling such as myself and working through them was a long and laborious process, but just to see movement where there previously had been none, was exciting. Every minor change inspired me on to continue my exercises with more vigor and vim.

When I wasn't in a session, I would make time in my room to continue exercising my muscles every day. I would push back with my legs while sitting in my wheelchair. At first, the movement was negligible. After a while, I actually got a small propulsion out of it. I also used elastic bands to increase my arm strength. Soon I was able to adjust my rear end in my wheelchair seat unaided. I couldn't stand, but I could adjust. That was nothing short of spectacular! No longer did I have to call in a staff member when my bum felt sore. I could now adjust myself in a flash and keep on going. And thanks to my airbeds in the hospital and at the rehab center, and the air-cushion seat on my wheelchair, I had no pressure sores to contend with.

Eventually, I worked my way up to 1 lb. weights. Then I started focusing on curls and arm extensions. I must have looked like an absolute weakling, but for me, it was all I could do. Sheila and Andrea just kept encouraging me and working my muscles.

The staff started to look at me differently since I slowly started gaining movement and could assist in my transfers. Carol, an aide there, said to me one night after dinner, "This is so weird. You came in here a full lift without any ability to help yourself. Now you're moving on your own and able to help with the Sabina. It's amazing."

I still didn't have great range of motion in my arms and my shoulders. So I needed help to wipe after a bowel movement, and I needed help in the shower to get myself clean. It's very humbling to have people around you during these traditionally private times. Your natural reaction is to request privacy and close doors when you need a bathroom break or when a shower is desired. So to have someone help you onto the toilet and then come back in when you're done to flush the toilet and wipe you up is quite un-nerving. And for the staff, they acted like "it's just part of my job." They didn't seem to mind the activities requested.

Over time, I began to gain more range in my arm and shoulders and was finally able to wipe myself. That was liberating, to say the least. Staff still had to get me in and out of the bathroom, and I needed them to undress me and re-dress me once I was finished, but I didn't have to ask anyone to wipe up after me.

The process was slow, but improvements came. I began to move my legs without assistance. My fidgeting habit quickly began to reappear. My wife, who never liked it when my legs fidgeted, was annoyingly surprised when she saw it return. I just looked at her and said, "whatever muscles I can move, I'm gonna move!" She tolerated it only slightly more than before.

With the aid of the adjustable bed, I began to get myself to the side of the bed without assistance. That way, when the technician came in, they only had to help me get into my wheelchair and I was good for the day. I still urinated in a urinal I kept beside my wheelchair, but now I had the ability to empty it on my own into the toilet. I still had to call someone over to fill my water container, because I didn't have the strength to remove the top cover yet. But that would come in time.

Throughout this time of muscle growth and strengthening, I still had my blood sugars to deal with. Being on steroids kept my sugars in flux. They never stabilized no matter how much my diet remained the same. One morning I woke up with a 48 blood sugar. I didn't even feel different. But I knew that was a risky level to be at, so I quickly got some sugar in me and continued on my day. In the afternoon times, my blood sugars would range anywhere from 140 to 350. I purposefully didn't take in any other food than what the rehab facility provided. Still, nothing could combat the steroid effect on my sugar levels. So I got a lot of insulin during my stay.

I'm surprised at the things that catch your attention when you're ill. I had lost significant weight during my hospital stay. I wasn't thin, I was emaciated. My bones were easy to see beneath the skin. Nothing hid my ribs from view. My arms and legs looked like sticks. And what did I notice getting dressed from a shower? I no longer had a "belly." My abdomen was finally flat! I hadn't had a flat abdomen since I played football in high school. I remember smiling to myself and thinking, "Great! I'll never get that back again!"

Well, I found out that insulin can make you gain abdominal weight. And that was exactly the first thing that came back once I started gaining weight. Even though the rest of me was still stick-like, my belly began to show again. I thought it would start at my chest and work out from there, but no! There it was for all the world to see. And without any chest muscles, it was only that much bigger!

It wasn't long before I came to my senses. Here I was, suffering from a major disease. I had died and come back and now I was in a nursing home trying to get out of a wheelchair, and all I could think about was belly fat! It amazed me how quickly I focused on such a trivial thing.

I slowly started getting around my room by pushing myself backwards in the wheelchair with my legs. They were stronger than my arms, though that wasn't saying much. But it kept my muscles growing.

When Karen or other family members came by, I would occasionally get a walk around the grounds, or at least out to the front area of the facility. It was quite a change from my "normal life" of being able to go wherever I desired and do whatever I cared. Instead, though I was allowed out of my room, I rarely ever left it because I fatigued easily. And I really never left the building unless accompanied by someone else, lest I fatigue outside and there would be no one there to help me.

CHAPTER TWENTY-SIX

Praising God Through the Trials

Every morning when I woke up, I would start the day by going to my Bible app and reading the suggested passages on the "Read thru the Bible in a year" portion. I felt God speaking to me thru those daily scripture readings. And sometimes in the oddest ways. One day, I read about king Nebuchadnezzar and how God dealt with him. In Daniel (4:28-37), it tells about the king taking credit for all of the glory in his kingdom. "While the word was in the king's mouth, a voice came from heaven, saying, 'King Nebuchadnezzar, to you it is declared: sovereignty has been removed from you, and you will be driven away from mankind, and your dwelling place will be with the beasts of the field. You will be given grass to eat like cattle, and seven periods of time will pass over you until you recognize that the Most High is ruler over the realm of mankind and bestows it on whomever He wishes.'"

The king immediately went out and began eating in the field like an animal and his hair and nails grew out. After a period of time, his reason was restored to him. I thought about the fact that he was king over Babylon. He was used to getting anything he desired and all of a sudden had it taken away. He knew who did this to him. After all, it was prophesied to him and openly told to him so he would know why this happened.

Now I would expect a guy like the king to be mad at anyone who would do such a thing to him. But instead, the Bible describes how King Nebuchadnezzar praised

God afterwards. In light of my situation, I began to understand why he reacted the way he did. God brought me to this time in my life in a miraculous way and showed me He had His hand on me throughout my experience. Nebuchadnezzar knew God was real when He spoke openly to him.

Once God makes His presence real to you, you understand His power and sovereignty. You realize quickly it is better to be suffering through a moment of trial and be in His will, than to be living like a king outside of His will. Being in His will is better than anything this world can offer. That is why Nebuchadnezzar praised God after his trial, and I could praise him throughout mine.

When my strength began to return, many were surprised to see it. I began to lift my arms off of the wheelchair arm rests. After that, I found I could lift my knees up in the air about two inches. That was tremendous! I showed my family, and they were shocked. Knowing what I was like in the hospital, they were shocked that I was getting movement back so fast.

I would practice getting out of my wheelchair daily. But the best I could do was to lift my butt off of the cushion ever so slightly. I just didn't have the strength to get beyond that point. Many days later, I went to get up, and actually found myself standing! I had always placed a table in front of my wheelchair in case I fell forward during my attempts. But I didn't fall. Instead I was out of my chair and standing between it and the table. It was then that I knew I didn't have long to go before I would be able to leave the facility.

The next day I couldn't wait to show Andrea, my physical therapy tech, my latest accomplishment. She was very pleased and stunned! "I'm going to get you a walker and we'll start working with it," she said with a smile. Sheila, my occupational therapy tech, was equally pleased at my progress. "We'll keep working those arms so they can support you on your walker." These improvements helped encourage me to work out all the more.

One day while listening to the T.V., I overheard someone as their mother was being released early from prison. "God is good," he said. It reminded me of a phrase often used by churchgoers, "God is good – All the time." I hear it more often quoted during prosperous times, like when someone gets a new job or promotion. Or when a loved one comes out of a hospital stay or other trial all right.

Though we're quick to remember the first part of the phrase, we rarely remember the second part, "All the time." God is not good because of our circumstance. God is good because of His character. His plans are always for our benefit (Jer. 29:11-13). If we follow in His ways, He will make sure things work out for our good (Rom. 8:28). Though we may not see how God is working out our current problem, we do know His promises. Now, when problems arise, I pray, "God, please show me my part in Your plan today. What do You want me to learn? How do You want me to glorify You through this trial?" In doing that, it gets my mind off of the trial and onto God and His will for me. It also helps to remember to say, "God is good – All the time" when a trial comes your way. That helps to get the focus away from you and your trial and get back to where it belongs, on God and your relationship with Him.

Andrea started taking me to the PT gym room by way of a walker. She would have me use the walker while she walked behind me pushing the wheelchair. That way, if I ever got fatigued, she would have the wheelchair at the ready for me. Early on, that was a blessing, because I did fatigue easily. But after a few days, I was walking to the P.T. gym without the need for the wheelchair to accompany me. To say the staff was surprised would be an understatement! I was the guy who came into the facility unable to move from side to side in bed. Now I was walking down the halls easily with a walker.

Both Andrea and Sheila continued to push me during my PT and OT sessions. Andrea practiced with me getting up from a sitting position from chairs of varying heights. "Always position your hands on the arm rests before you get up or sit down," she frequently reminded me. Sheila continued to give me arm-strengthening tasks, such as pushing her away while she was seated on a rolling stool (which I began to accomplish more easily). She would also use weights to build up my arm strength. That made getting out of chairs much easier.

My strength grew almost daily. I began to take on other tasks, like going up and down stairs. I was also taken outside and walked on uneven surfaces. My wife brought my home walker to the nursing home (which included a built-in seat, if needed). I felt like I was living high on the hog with that upgraded walker.

It was eventually decided that July 28th of 2015 would be my departure date back home. Eric, the night nurse, on the night before my departure, brought me my last ensure smoothie and said, "Well, all you have is the 'wake up' and you're home-free." Being ex-navy he made that comment to remind me of a common military term. When stationed overseas, you often knew exactly how long you would be staying on a given base before you would fly back to the USA. We would refer to it as the number of full days you had left plus the day you would "wake up" for the last time on base and fly away. So if someone asked you how long you "have left," you'd say, "65 days and a wake-up."

I laughed at Eric because I hadn't heard that term in many years. "I wish I had remembered that earlier," I said. "I would have been using that phrase for many days now." We then spoke about where our lives were headed and some of our military past. It was funny, because now I was saying goodbye to some individuals who I had grown close to during my time at the rehab facility. It felt a bit like a graduation from school and saying goodbye to those you might not see again.

The next morning, that situation played itself out over and over again. I spoke with the technicians who came to me. A few didn't have business in my room but made it a point to come by and give their regards. They were very honest in their kind words to me and I was very surprised how many said they enjoyed taking care of me.

Later that morning, my wife arrived, and we began packing up my personal items and getting it in the car. Then I took a final walk down the hallway and waved goodbye to those around me. We got into the car and then headed to a local restaurant to grab a lunch. Getting in and out of the place was a small challenge for me, not being accustomed to working around "normal" bustling individuals. But everything went well. The food tasted good and I almost felt "normal" myself for the first time in a long time.

When we finally got back home, Karen and I took our time getting me inside the house. Using the front door was difficult, since the steps were tall, and the floor was uneven. Instead, we went through the garage. When I last left my home many months earlier, our garage was packed with all kinds of stuff and was quite impassable. Now, the stuff was all gone (moved to other locations) and was easy for me to make it inside the house that way. Once inside, Karen had the wheelchair ready for me and I used that to initially get around from one room to the next. I also used the walker quite a bit. The more I used my legs, the more I could trust them to hold me up.

My family had prepared a spare room and turned it into a new bedroom for me on the first floor. They put a single size adjustable bed in there and gave me a hospital bed table to use for computer work and other activities. I couldn't roll a wheelchair into it, but I could get my walker in there without much problem. When I came out of my room, I would use the walker to get into (and out of) the bathroom, and to get me to my wheelchair. I would then use the wheelchair to get around the rest of the first floor.

CHAPTER TWENTY-SEVEN

Out and About

My first scheduled Physical Therapy out-patient appointment came the following week. I went to the same place I had gone to prior to being admitted several months previously. Kathy, my old P.T. tech, was there and she couldn't believe my progress. Before, she needed help getting me from the wheelchair to the padded table. Every movement was done with very little ability on my part, and significant effort on her part.

Now, I was able to transfer by myself, though slowly and without much finesse. My muscles were still weak, but stronger than the last time I was here. She just stared at me in amazement for a while. "Wow, I just can't believe how far you've come since I last saw you!" I caught her up on all that had happened to me in the hospital and what I was now capable of doing. She retested my new condition and began putting me through workouts to help improve my strength. Looking at her look at me was kind of fun, because even I didn't fully appreciate how far I came until I saw her trying to process my new condition in her head.

I was jerky and slow in my movements, but I did move on my own. Each time I came for a visit, she would up my activities a bit. She worked on me getting me up from a supine position. Even with the use of my arms, this was a very difficult task. Then she had me pick up small items from off of the floor, like paper. Again, hard to do without strong leg and core muscles. She would also run me through workouts on weight machines to help build strength.

After a few sessions, she began working with me on getting up and down stairs. They had a group of five or six stairs that led nowhere but allowed one to practice with them carefully. Once that task got easier, she took me to a real set of stairs that went to a downstairs location. Using a cane, she got me to practice going down them and back up again, tasks that sound fairly easy to the average individual, but were quite challenging for me.

Eventually, she started changing my mode of ambulation. "I want you to start using a walking stick wherever you go. It allows you to provide yourself stability as you walk, and it puts you in a more upright position than a regular cane would." "Plus that," she said, "it makes you look more adventuresome than a cane does." Quite the sales pitch, I thought. So I put the walker aside and bought a walking stick the Friday she spoke to me about changing.

Getting around with the walking stick wasn't too difficult. It gave me good balance and was easy to tuck away once I got to where I was going. If I were headed to a large store, I would use the walking stick to get me from the car to the store, and then I would transfer to one of the store's battery-operated transporters. That system worked great for me.

The following Monday, I met with Kathy again. She went over a few exercises with me. "You know, you seem to have gained strength even just over the weekend. I think you're ready to give up the walking stick." "What?" I exclaimed. "I haven't even worn out the warranty on this thing yet." I wasn't sure about giving up the walking stick just yet, but I trusted her. So, reluctantly, I tried to go everywhere without using any additional walking helps. I was nervous at first, but I gained strength and courage each passing day.

For large stores, I still used the battery-operated transporters because they were easier for me than walking throughout the store. Then one day, while in shorts, I noticed I had no calf muscles to speak of as I was getting out of the transporter. It dawned on me that if I wasn't going to walk around and use my leg muscles, I would never grow my leg muscles. "Honey," I told my wife, "I think I'm going to have to skip these transporters and just walk like regular through the stores." Though it was harder for me to walk through the store, it was better for my overall health taking on the more challenging task.

I saw a spiritual truth in my trials, another epiphany, if you will (epiphany #5). Just like physical muscles, if you don't work your spiritual muscles, you'll never grow them. In other words, if you don't keep reading God's word and keep in prayer, it's easy to get farther away from those activities and from God's presence. My muscles would never grow unless I used them and used them frequently. If I didn't follow God in the simple things, why would God trust me with greater tasks and challenges?

Often, we feel that if we give God our Sunday mornings and some money in the offering plate, then we've done "our part" to commune with God. But the Bible says, "To obey is better than sacrifice." (Isa. 15:22.). God desires us to be willing to do whatever He asks of us. Even if it seems hard to do at the time. For me, walking was not an easy (or graceful) task. Yet, if I didn't do it, I'd never grow in strength or agility.

So, I bypassed the transporters and began walking

throughout the stores. At first, this was very taxing on my abilities. Walking was not an effortless process for me. And after about 10 minutes, I would find myself looking for a place to sit down. Most stores didn't have rest areas, so I was forced to stay on my feet. As my muscles grew, standing became less of an inconvenience and more of a "normal" activity.

The hardest muscles to regrow have been my chest and upper back muscles. I started going to the gym and using rowing machines and weight machines to regrow muscles. That helped some, but in trying to find time to do basic activities, like interacting with friends and family, and allowing time for work, and being available to write this book, I had to forsake a lot of gym time. So as of this writing, my chest and back muscles are still not where they were prior to my condition. I mean, I can definitely lift heavier items than when I was recently discharged from the hospital, but I still ask my wife for help when opening tight jars.

CHAPTER TWENTY-EIGHT

Gifts from God

One area of early disappointment came in my inability to sing or play music. I have been in church choirs and worship teams almost my entire life. I would sing both melodies and harmonies and play either rhythm guitar, bass guitar, or drums. When my disease occurred, I lost vocal cord and diaphragm muscle. I found I could no longer hit or hold a note. My speaking voice had a frog-like tenor to it. And as for instruments, I lost the ability to hold an instrument for any great length of time and play with determination.

This was disheartening to me. I felt my musical talents were a gift from God and I used it primarily in church to honor Him. So I was having a tough time understanding why God would take this talent from me. Then I remembered what Job said when he lost his property and his family all in one day. "...The Lord gave and the Lord has taken away. Blessed be the name of the Lord" (Job 1:21b).

This was another epiphany for me (epiphany #6). If God gives you a gift, understand it may only be for a brief time. Often, I hear people claiming to be "mad at God" for no longer being able to do what they previously could do. Instead of being thankful for the time they had the gift, they sometimes even use it as an excuse to turn their back on God. It's as if they feel God does not have the right to be sovereign in their lives.

Though music was a very big part of my life, I knew God knew my heart and was in control of all things. So I prayed and told the Lord, "Thank you for the gift of music you gave me to use. I don't understand why You took it away, but please show me what You want me to do, and how You want me to serve You from now on." It allowed me to keep my eyes focused on what mattered. It wasn't important that I could no longer sing and play. What was important was that I continued to love God and serve God as best I could.

As I continued to regain muscle, I eventually was able to pick the guitar back up and help on the church worship team once again. Eventually, I also got back on drums and bass guitar as the team needed. Now, in spite of my voice being only partially back, I'm even able to sing along with the group. My abilities are returning slowly, but they are coming back.

This has been miraculous to the congregation who saw me previously in a wheelchair, unable to even move the chair on my own. Gradually, they saw me using a walker, and then a walking stick. Now I'm back to walking unaided by any additional supports. And when they see me play the drums, I often have parishioners come up to me and comment on how they can't believe I'm moving my arms and legs like I am!

CHAPTER TWENTY-NINE

Getting Back in the Saddle

Many of the surgeons who work with me saw me while I was in the hospital and when I was on a ventilator. They saw how fast I lost muscle mass and ability. They said they would hold my job for me, but I heard later on that many of them expected I would not live through this disease.

When I returned in early October of 2015, they could hardly believe I was the same guy they saw just a few months earlier clinging to life in the ICU. The week before I returned to work, I visited my workplace to talk about coming back and I walked in unaided. I still remember Dr. Magillicutty staring at me in quizzical amazement as I spoke with the staff and walked about unaided. He had last seen me about two months prior, when I still could not get around without a wheelchair. Now, absorbing all of the recent changes that occurred, he looked at me like someone trying to figure out how a magician performed a spectacular trick right in front of his eyes! It was great to know that God really did a miraculous thing in my life.

Those who didn't know about my condition or see me when I was very ill, just looked at me like I was a normal person. That, also, was a fun thing; because for the longest time, I was looked at as "handicapped." People tried to either look away when I was out around town, or they would talk to me as if English were a second language for me. They would speak slowly to me or overly enunciate each word. So being treated like I used to be treated was great.

Since my Loveland office was on the second floor, I originally used the elevator to go up there and I entered through the front door. As I began to gain strength, I went back to using the back stairs to get to my office. I often had to pause halfway up to make it to the top, but I did make it. Eventually, as my leg muscles improved, I was once again able to climb the stairs with minimal difficulty.

As of this writing, I'm still not back to 100% full strength. My legs feel stiff and cumbersome whenever I've spent time in a seated position. So after driving from home to work, and when I return home, I get out of the car with a bit of effort and my gait is slow to start. It usually takes me a few minutes before I'm able to have a decent stride going.

My arms are still weak from my disease. Since I don't use them as much, the muscles have yet to grow completely back. Fortunately, my work doesn't require I possess a great deal of muscular prowess.

Things have started to return to normal. I no longer require a walker, cane, or any other ambulatory support in order to get around. My patients don't look at me any differently than any other provider they see. People who meet me seem to think I'm just another normal joe. Occasionally, one of my medical assistants will bring it up when someone is giving me a bit of friendly grief at work. "Hey, cut him a little slack. You know he died last year." To which I'll usually chime in, "Yeah. It's not easy coming back from oblivion." Then we'll all laugh about it.

CHAPTER THIRTY

He Holds the Future

We often wonder if God thinks about us or really has control of our lives. But for me, the biggest miracle came years before my illness. I was working for a urology clinic in 2011 and pulling between 50-65 hours every week. I would get to the hospital before clinic and make rounds on our surgical patients. If needed, I would discharge them from the hospital and get their prescriptions ready when they left.

After that, I would rush over to the clinic and see the patients scheduled for me that day. If a consult request came to the clinic, they would usually send me over to the hospital to do it. On surgery days, I would be the 1st Assistant in the OR and would make pre-op and post-op rounds on the patients. I would also write their post-op orders while the surgeons were dictating their operative reports. After work, I would go back to the hospital and make evening rounds on any of our patients. And I also pulled 12-13 days of call every month, answering phone calls through the night from patients and the hospital. The hours were long and the pay was unchanged, regardless of any additional work performed. I felt somewhat abused.

One day in October of 2011, I got a consult to visit a patient on the pediatric floor. This was rare for urology, since most urologic problems were associated with the elderly. The fact of the matter was the hospital had maxed out their bed space, so they had actually put an elderly patient on the pediatric floor.

It had been so long since I had been there, I had to look the location up. So I went there and met with the patient and evaluated him for his urinary flow problems. I then took a seat out near the nurses' station and began writing my report in the chart. Along came a doctor I hadn't seen in over 3-4 years. He was Dr. Frank Roberts. The last time I saw him, he was a resident MD and had come to our clinic to learn urology. We got along well, and it was good seeing him again.

"Dr. Roberts, as I live and breathe. What brings you out here on this fine day?" "Well," he said, "I never come out to the peds floor, but I'm on call for family practice and one of the docs needs this kid seen, so here I am." "Hey," I chimed in, "I never come here either. What a coincidence." "By the way," he continued, "If you know of any PAs that might be looking for work, let me know, because I'm interested in hiring someone."

Suddenly, I began to hear a voice in my head say, "This is no coincidence. I brought you two together here where neither of you usually come." "Well," I casually mentioned, "It not exactly Nirvana where I'm at. So, what do you got going?" He looked seriously at me and then came and sat down beside me. Quickly we began discussing his situation. "I'm opening up a new family practice clinic in town and I'd love to have you come on board." "You'd get two exam rooms to yourself and we have lab facilities in-house. You'd have 1-2 techs to keep your schedule going and a procedure room is available whenever you need it."

The voice in my head began saying, "It's time for you to leave your job." That was odd, since I hadn't thought much about it before. I mean, yeah, it was a hard job to do, but this clinic taught me all I know about urology, so I felt I owed them something. But I had been there for a total of 8 years already. And they didn't seem eager to change my working situation any time soon.

Well, as for compensation, he offered me the lion's share of what I bring into the company. This would be a considerable pay increase from just routine salary. Then the voice really started getting loud and clear: "Do you hear what he's telling you? Do you see this meeting I arranged for you? It's time to leave your current job."

So, I told him I'd like to look at his new clinic and also talk it over with my wife. He said "great." "Now, let me go check on this kid and I'll be right back." Two minutes later he came back. "Wow, this kid is being seen by his pediatrician. I didn't even need to be here today. How about that?" Again, the voice said, "Did you hear that? He didn't even need to be here. I arranged this meeting. You need to leave your job."

A few days later, we met in his new office. Final additions were happening and the place had that new clinic smell. It was very well organized, and I could see myself working in a facility like this. I had ample room for my activities, and support areas were well staffed and ready to go. Again, I was impressed by what was being offered.

"OK," I said. "I'm in. But I'll have to give my current clinic fair notice. Let's plan on me working through December at my current job and starting with you the first week of January." "That sounds good," he agreed. "That should give us enough time to get your credentials in order before you start."

Well, I went back to my clinic and informed my office manager what I decided. Then, I got with each surgeon individually and informed them about my leaving. Each one of them said they thought I was making a big mistake in leaving the clinic, but they would honor my request. They were glad I could stay with them through the end of December. I even said I'd be happy to train my replacement if they came in time.

So, throughout November and December, I spent a lot of my free time filling out forms and mailing credentialing information to all who requested it. I also started telling my current patients that I would be leaving the practice for a family medicine position in town, if they needed any family practice support.

Things were going well, but the day after Christmas, I got a call from Dr. Roberts. "Dave, can you come by my office when you get off work today?" "Sure," I replied. After work, I went over to see him. He looked a bit bothered, so we went into his office. "Dave, I'm sorry but I can't hire you right now." "What," I exclaimed? "All of my credentials are expiring at the end of the month. I worked hard to make this a smooth transition. What's the problem?"

"Well," he began, "I'm under litigation for the name of my clinic. The hospital wants me to change my name and I'm not about to roll over for those buffoons. So, they're taking me to court. The money I was going to use to hire you, I now have to use to acquire attorneys. So, I have to let you go."

I was shocked! I felt strongly that God opened this door for me. Now I was standing in front of a door that was just slammed in my face! I would be unemployed in 4 days and I had no other jobs waiting for me in the wings. This was indeed a tough spot to be in.

I really didn't know what to make of it all. I began to go over in my head what had previously transpired to get me here. Every time I thought about the meeting on the pediatric floor and all that was said, I knew the voice of the Lord was speaking to me then. I knew I would come to the same conclusions even now.

But I had no job, and I was running out of time and options fast. I spoke to my wife about it and told her what recently occurred. I felt my only option was to go back to my current clinic, hat-in-hand so to speak, and see if they might allow me to work there a few more months while I found out where I would be heading next. "After all," I thought, "the surgeons all said they thought I was making a big mistake. I bet they'd love to have me back for a bit longer." Not a chance! I upset them by wanting to leave their office. Besides, I felt God saying, "I told you I want you out of that job." So each of them said, "You asked us to leave, and we're going to honor your request. Take care."

I couldn't get mad at them, because they did what I originally asked them to do, they let me go. So I went home and prayed. I asked God to find me the job he wanted me to be in. Then I started canvasing the classified pages of the local paper, and the regional and federal job sites out and around for anything I could get into. In the past, I had done some temporary work in my field, called "locums" work. I called the old locums company and asked if they could use me. They informed me they didn't have any urology PA positions right now, and they could only use me for family practice if I had done family medicine in the last 2 years (which I hadn't).

Then, two weeks into January, a nurse I used to work with, called me and told me a urology clinic she used to be at in Loveland, Colorado, was looking for a PA and she thought I would be a good fit down there. I called them up and immediately got an interview with them. I went over and met with a few of the surgeons there and brought along my reference information. They were pleased with what I brought and agreed to hire me. They agreed to pay me $5,000 more a year, but otherwise, it was a very similar hiring package as to what the Cheyenne clinic offered.

Since I wasn't licensed in Colorado yet, they began working on my license for me and credentialing paperwork for the hospitals I would be assisting in surgery. This process was going to take a few months, and I was burning through my bank account just to make ends meet. Fortunately, a locums company I hadn't heard of before, offered me a position in South Dakota working for the Indian Health Service. They needed someone ASAP to help with a shortage they were experiencing in a small town called Eagle Butte.

The nice thing about working for the government was that they only required I be licensed in a state, they didn't care which one it was. I verified my license with Dr. Roberts would still be good and I called my new clinic and informed them I would be out of town for a few months while the credentialing process continued. Everyone was OK with what was happening.

When I called the South Dakota locums company, they said, "Now remember, Eagle Butte is very rural." "OK," I replied. "No big deal." "Yes," they reiterated. "It is a big deal. You're going to fill in for a locums PA who was supposed to stay there for 3 months, but only lasted a week, due to isolation issues. We've got to know you can manage isolation." "Dude," I began, "I spent 20 years in the Air Force, and I've been to a few isolated areas in my life. I'm sure I can handle Eagle Butte."

So we agreed to the deal on Tuesday, and I was in route to Eagle Butte that weekend to begin work on

Monday. The place was in the north-central area of South Dakota, away from any large town. There was a Dairy Queen and a Subway in town, but the nearest McDonald's was about one and a half hours away. The supermarket in town was small and a Family Dollar store was the primary business for getting routine supplies.

The hospital was fairly new and had nice clinic and in-patient facilities. They had also built a small neighborhood of duplexes out back for visiting medical staff to use while in-town. Jim, one of the staff folks helping me acclimate said, "Be careful not to go for long walks at night." "Why? Do you have street gangs out here," I chuckled? "No, but we do have wild dogs that roam around in packs and they will attack you." Ok, I thought. Wild dogs were a new concern I hadn't had to deal with before.

The town was located in the Cheyenne River Sioux Reservation. It actually wound up being a wonderful place to work. The people were friendly and the support for the family practice clinic was good. I even enjoyed getting back into family practice for a while. Having been a family practice provider for over nine years and having to maintain my family practice national board certification as a PA in general, it wasn't a great stretch doing family medicine once again. It was like the proverbial bicycle riding; easy on, easy off.

Money started coming back into the account, and once again I began paying my bills. Eventually, I was notified that my Colorado credentials were about complete, so I gave my notice at the IHS facility and headed home to Cheyenne.

I started working at the Loveland urology clinic in Mid-June of 2012. The drive was about 50 minutes each way, but there was no need for doing in-patient rounds or pulling call. My nights and weekends were mine. I even started getting books on tape from the library and listened to them while driving. That was relaxing and educational at the same time. I found the freeway between my house and my work to be mostly vacant of other vehicles during my travel, so I could always go at a fairly good speed and make it home easily by dinner.

Well, three months after I joined the practice, they were bought out by the University of Colorado Health. The new company came in and spoke to each of the providers separately. Mary, one of the provider support staff, discussed the new package deal with me. "We treat all of our providers the same, so you'll start getting quarterly RVU (work activity) bonuses just like the MDs do." I had never received anything more than Christmas bonuses in the past, so all I could say was, "Thanks." "Oh," she continued, "you also will have disability insurance along with your other benefits." I hadn't heard that term before and had no clue as to what it was all about. "OK," was all I could produce for a reply.

That all happened in September/October timeframe of 2012. Fast forward to April 2015 and the disability insurance I hardly thought about at the time it came to me, saved my financial situation once I became ill and unable to work. It provided me full pay and benefits while I was in the hospital. While I required medical staff to do everything for me, I was still getting paid like I had never left work. Later on, when I checked back on my previous workplace in Cheyenne, I found out I had no disability insurance over there. Had I still been in my old job when my illness occurred, my income would have ceased once I quit working. That would have been devastating for me.

Originally, When God first told me to leave my current position, I assumed it was for a family practice position in my town, but it wasn't. He was telling me to leave where I was. That was it! I originally thought he was showing me His whole plan, but He was really just showing me my next step. I could have easily gotten mad at God when the plan (I assumed I knew) began to fall apart, but instead I realized His plan was to get me out of my job. He had yet to show me steps beyond that.

That lead me to another epiphany (epiphany #7), God often leads us one step at a time. Like Paul, the apostle, when he was first called on the road to Damascus (Acts 9), he was blinded by God, but was not told how long he would be blind or what all this was for. Instead, he was led into Damascus and told a man named Ananias would be visiting him soon. If we trust God and take the next step He's showing us, He will show us where to step after that.

Too often we say to God, "show me the whole plan so I can give my approval or voice my opinion on it before I follow You." That's not how God works. He wants us to trust in Him with all our heart first. Then He will guide your steps. (Pro. 3:5-6).

I recall seeing a news story while I was in the hospital. A 30-something year old man had suffered a serious shoulder and hip injury from a motorcycle accident. He incurred significant medical bills from all the treatments he underwent. He was at a collectables shop selling his sports cards to help raise money for his mounting medical bills. I thought, "There, but for the grace of God, go I." Without the disability insurance, I would have been right next to him selling off whatever I could to make ends meet.

Now, my bills were being paid, and insurance was

covering all of my therapies. I realize that when I took this job, disability insurance wasn't even offered to me and I didn't know enough to even ask about it. So there was no way this package was sought out by me or even available to me if I had known what to ask for. It all came after I joined.

My new work group was also very kind to me. When I first got sick, the corporation said they would maintain my job until July 7th, three months from the start of my time off. When that time had come and gone, I met with a few of the surgeons while I was still an in-patient. I informed them that I knew I could not go back to work in the allotted time, and I would understand if they had to hire someone else to fill my empty seat. "No," they said. "We like you and think you're a good fit for our clinic. We'll hold your position for you until you come back."

I promised them I wouldn't consider coming back until "I can walk into a room and nobody's thinking about my health." I cleared that hurdle in late September 2015. I had quit using any walking aids and looked fairly normal in strength and activity. Roughly 6 months after this odyssey began, I returned to work, and my disability insurance ended. I walked into work feeling weak, but "normal."

It amazes me that, even though I had no clue as to what was coming up in my life, God knew and got me to a job and position that allowed me to go through this without any significant financial burden. I remember telling my wife, "I'm glad this happened to me and not one of our friends. If it had happened to one of them and they weren't adequately insured, it would have been devastating for them." Not that it wasn't challenging for me, but all I had to do was live through it. The insurances

I carried helped with any financial issues.

Since coming back to the clinic, I have continued to grow in strength. I've been going to the gym and trying to keep active. I've extended my appointment time to ½ hour intervals and my patients love the extra time I spend with them addressing their problems. My job, fortunately, doesn't require a lot of muscle power to perform, so I'm able to keep up without much problem.

I used to use the handicapped parking because I couldn't walk very far. Now, I feel strong enough to park wherever there's space. Walking is not a problem for me. I still occasionally ask for help with things that require grip strength, such as twisting a lid off a jar, or opening a bottle. My hands are strong, but not like before.

My final epiphany came later in my ordeal. As I mentioned earlier, Jeremiah 1:5 states, "Before I formed you in the womb I knew you, and before you were born I consecrated you…" Often, we think we have a soul. I don't believe that's the case. I believe we ARE a soul! What we have is a body! (Epiphany #8) Before our bodies were formed, God knew us. What was present before our bodies were formed? Our souls! Why is that important? Well, it puts our existence in perspective.

Did you know there are no pharmacies or hospitals in heaven? Why is that? Because those places are needed to correct issues related to our bodies. Throughout our lives, our bodies acquire injuries, maladies, and deformities. They are mortal and designed to decay over time. We use them here on earth as a transportation device and a means of interacting with other things while on this planet.

But when we leave earth, our bodies will no longer be needed and will remain here. We, the soul, will be called away. Keeping that in mind, verses such as John 11:25

become more understandable. "Jesus said unto her, I am the resurrection and the life: he that believeth in me, though he were dead, yet shall he live:" (KJV).

For those of us who are going through challenges with our bodies, take heart! These issues are for a short time only. When you leave this earth, all of your physical diseases and conditions stay with your body. You do not take them with you! "For I consider that the sufferings of this present time are not worthy to be compared with the glory that is to be revealed to us." (Rom. 8:18 NASB).

CHAPTER THIRTY-ONE

Earthy-land

I was raised in Southern California during the 60s and the 70s. Part of that time, I even lived a mile and a half from Disneyland. Ticket prices were not as expensive back then as they are now. Because of that, it was not out of the question to occasionally hear about a parent dropping off their kids at the front gate, letting everybody out, throwing some money their way, and telling them; "Ok, kids. Go ride on all the rides, see all the sites, and eat at the restaurants. We'll be back to pick you up before it closes." Then the parents would take off and leave the kids unattended at the amusement park while they had the day to themselves.

I think some people believe God is a bit like that. He pulled up to the entrance to "Earthy-Land" in His big pick-up truck, threw some money at us, and said, "Ok, kids. Go ride on all the rides, see all the sites, and have a fun time. I have to do some construction work on the mansion. I'll be back to pick you all up before it closes." You hear it often in the way people discuss their "bucket list" of things to do before they die. "I want to visit every continent and try the different cuisine offerings." "I want to see the seven wonders of the world in person." "I want to climb every mountain."

Now don't get me wrong. There are times when we need rest. There are instances where we need to spend time bonding with family and friends. But we should look, even in those restful times, for opportunities to share our faith with others. We too easily get caught up in the things around us. Romans 12:2 (NASB) states, "And do not be conformed to this world, but be transformed by the renewing of your mind, so that you may prove what the will of God is, that which is good and acceptable and perfect." God did not send us here to see all the sites and ride all the rides. He brought us here to seek after Him, to choose Him as our Lord and Savior, to learn how we can live our life and handle our challenges through Him, and to help others to find God.

We must learn to look beyond what is around us and see the spiritual issues happening in front of us. As I mentioned previously, if you are looking at the physical, you're looking in the wrong place! "Set your mind on the things above, not on the things that are on earth." (Col. 3:2) (NASB)

I believe earth is more a spiritual proving ground for us Christians to work on our faith. Somewhat like a spiritual basic training. We train here to work out our faith for things that will happen to us both later in life here and in the age to come.

But some of us even lose site of that analogy. Instead of understanding the temporary purpose of our time here on earth, we get caught up in making our time here most comfortable. It's like being in the military basic training and a fellow recruit shows great aptitude in basic. Then they come to you and say, "I like this basic stuff. I really enjoy marching and inspections, and the confidence course activities. I think I'm going to spend my entire 4 years right here in basic. I'll get a place off base and come into base each morning to start my day."

It wouldn't take but a moment before someone smacked him upside the back of the head and said, "hey numb skull, this is not the real world. This is basic training. It's preparing you for the things you're going to have to do out there! Out there is the real world. Get with the program."

Sometimes you want to say something similar when you see Christians getting comfortable here on earth. "This isn't life. This is spiritual life prep. Eternal life starts once we leave here. That's when the real life begins."

Recently, God brought a verse to my recall: "I can do all things through Him who strengthens me." (Phil. 4:13) (NASB) A familiar verse I had heard many times before. Then He casually asked, "So Dave, how many "all things" are you doing through Me?" "I beg Your pardon?" That was all I could muster, being caught off-guard by the query. "Well," He said, "you say you can do all things through Me. I'm just wondering if you're actually trying to do "all things" through me?

Remember, God never asks you a question so he can know you better and understand you more completely. He already knows all your thoughts and actions. He asks you questions to help you understand yourself better! "Well, I usually work you into the big decisions like what car or house to buy. That kind of thing."

Then I heard Him say, "No Dave. I'm training you to do ALL THINGS through Me! Include Me in all your decisions of the day; what clothes to wear, where to shop and eat, what turns to make, etc. I will guide you to where I want you to be and where you can serve Me and My children."

I recall reading once about a man who had lost a daughter at an early age. One day, he saw a little girl wearing an outfit very similar to his daughter's style. It brought her back into his memory and made him smile. I think we often feel God is there just to bless us. But sometimes, through something as simple as the clothes we are wearing, God speaks to others in ways we don't even appreciate and provides them a blessing through us.

I have visited stores in the past and found myself behind someone unable to pay for their items. God prompted me to cover their cost and give them an unexpected blessing. Yes, it was for them God placed me there, but I also felt blessed in the interaction as well. I realize the more we converse with God through our day, the more He remains on our hearts and minds and guides us throughout our day.

CHAPTER THIRTY-TWO

The Potter and the Clay

I've learned a lot about God since going through this journey. I've learned that He is in control of all things and has seen all of our futures as the past. He gives us free will, and knows exactly what we'll do with our choices, even before we know. I know that Romans 8:28 promises that if we love God and are called according to His purpose, He will make everything turn out for our good. That isn't to say we will like everything that happens to us. It just means our obedience and faithfulness will be rewarded.

It's good to remember that God is the potter and we are the clay. He can mold us into anything He desires. Our goal is to allow Him to do that and to accept whatever role He desires for us to do. That's why Job, after having lost all of his possessions and family in one day said, "Though He slay me, I will hope in Him..." (Job 13:15). Job understood that God's desires alone mattered. God is God alone. Job needed to follow in God's plan and not try to focus on his own desires.

I think where we get off track is that we always look for immediate gratification, the "what's in it for me" attitude. If I can't see immediate benefit or self-gratification, then there is no desire for me to do it. But by only looking out for our needs, we miss what God has in store for us. "For I know the plans I have for you," declares the Lord, "plans for welfare and not for calamity to give you a future and a hope." (Jer. 29:11)

By putting God's desires above our own, we quickly

find that God's plans are just and that he will still work things out for our good in the end. He isn't guessing about the future like we are. He knows the future for He has seen it already in his past and he has total control over everything!

I've learned that if I ever have a problem or trial, I can go to God and say, "Why did You allow me to go through this?" "What do You want me to learn through this?" "How do You want me to glorify You in this?" Those simple questions help focus me on what really matters in this world – God! Remember, the physical is temporary. The spiritual is eternal. If we stay close to Him through trials and tribulations, nothing can touch us without His allowance or approval. Nothing! We are safe in His care!

I heard a friend recently say, "I've been getting to know God more recently through His word. The more I know God, the more I love God!" This ordeal has helped me know and love God more completely! With God at my side, I can face the world with much greater surety and hope!

The End

ABOUT THE AUTHOR

David R. Coleman, a urology physician assistant, has been in medicine since 1980 and a healthcare provider since 1992. He enlisted in the United States Air Force in 1980 and served as an operating room technician. He then became an officer in 1992 and retired from the USAF in 2000 as a physician assistant. During his career, he has been privileged to work as a PA in family practice, flight medicine, emergency medicine, urgent care, diabetes medicine, and urology. He has lectured nationally on many medical topics.

David has been active in his church communities since he began singing in choir during his elementary school years. He plays several instruments for his church worship team and serves as an elder there. David held the position of deacon in the past. He has a sincere heart for God that is evident throughout this book.

David presently resides in Wyoming with his wife, Karen.

For further information about Dave's journey, or to schedule him to speak at your church or group, contact him at throughthevalley@zoho.com.

Made in the USA
Las Vegas, NV
08 May 2023

71726716R00094